Jan Smedslund

Psycho-Logic

Springer-Verlag
Berlin Heidelberg New York
London Paris Tokyo

Professor Jan Smedslund
Institute of Psychology
University of Oslo
PB 1094, Blindern
0317 Oslo 3, Norway

ISBN 3-540-18518-6 Springer-Verlag Berlin Heidelberg New York
ISBN 0-387-18518-6 Springer-Verlag New York Berlin Heidelberg

Library of Congress Cataloging-in-Publication Data, Smedslund, Jan. Psycho-logic. Bibliography: p. 1. Psychology. I. Title.
BF121.S548   1988   150   87-37616
ISBN 0-387-18518-6 (U.S.)

Typesetting, printed and binding: Appl, Wemding
2126/3130-543210

To the ancient Greek geometers

Preface

In this work, I present the outcome of an attempt to explicate and systematize parts of *commonsense psychology,* that is, the psychology we all know tacitly and use in everyday life. This psychology is embedded in ordinary language and is acquired by everyone in the process of becoming socialized into a culture.

The book is dedicated to the ancient Greek geometers. They attempted to explicate the implicit structure of our spatial world. Without their achievements, the advance of the physical sciences, as we know them, could not have taken place. The present work is an effort to explicate the implicit structure of our psychological world. Without such an explication there can be no adequate scientific description and analysis of what persons experience and do. I hope this effort will have some value for the future advance of a psychological science.

Since what is presented is intended to consist only of common sense, it ought to be familiar and acceptable to every reader. Most of the specific propositions put forth have, at some time or other, been formulated by others. Hence, no claim to originality is made as far as the specific content is concerned. On the contrary, the number of people who have written things which correspond more or less to parts of what is presented here is very high. As a consequence of this, the task of giving references to all relevant publications has become entirely unmanageable, and, instead, I have decided to eliminate *all* references in the text. I think this break with convention is justified in view of the very special nature of the task, namely to explicate psychological common sense. Some readers may recognize *Spinoza, Fritz Heider, Alfred Schutz, Uwe Laucken,* and *Peter Ossorio* as being among the few who have had somewhat related global projects. I have profited from reading all of them. However, only Spinoza relied on the "geometric method," which is also used here.

In Appendix 3 there are some references to earlier presentations, critiques, and replies concerning the present type of approach. The term "psycho-logic" has been used by other authors. I am specifically aware of Abelson and Rosenberg (1958 – *Behavioral Science, 3,* 1–13) and Brandt (1982 – *Psychologists caught.* Toronto: University of Toronto Press). Abelson and Rosenberg focused on cognitive processing and equilibria, and Brandt studied the scientific and professional behavior of psychologists. Both these usages differ from the present one, where the term refers to the logical structure of the system of explicated psychological commonsense propositions.

Waldemar Rognes has read and commented on the entire manuscript in immensely helpful ways. He has also been a sympathetic and constructive ally and critic and has repeatedly assured me of the sanity of my undertaking. I certainly needed this during the first years, when international support was almost nonexistent. I would also like to mention Rognes's influence on the way in which I have defined the concept of feeling.

Ragnar Rommetveit, who has been a stimulating colleague and friend since we were students together, has also provided me with meticulous, sharp, and detailed criticism of the present work, for which I am deeply grateful.

My other colleagues at the Institute of Psychology in Oslo who have participated in the daily luncheon have provided me with a stimulating and warm human environment, with opportunities for trying out some of the formulations and for discussing the metatheoretical premises of the present project.

Much of the writing was done during the academic year 1985–1986 when I was a Visiting Scholar at the Department of Psychology, Stanford University. I am grateful for the opportunity to work undisturbed by ordinary teaching and administrative obligations. Also during that year, I talked regularly with *Leonard Horowitz, David Rosenhan,* and *Richard Shweder,* frequently about topics treated in the present book. I am indebted to them for the human and intellectual stimulation they provided. Finally, my wife *Åsebrit Sundquist* and our friends have made it easy for me to tolerate the relative isolation of my professional position. It has been a happy privilege to live in the midst of human contacts, even while pursuing a line of thought which, for a long time, was almost unanimously rejected by my colleagues in Norway and abroad.

Oslo, January 1988   *Jan Smedslund*

Contents

Contents

Introduction

Every science must have a language and every scientific language must be as precise as possible. This means that it should be possible for qualified scientists to infer, independently of each other, and with a high degree of intercorrelation, what other propositions follow from a given proposition, both in the direction of abstract formulations and in the direction of descriptions of actual events.

In psychology, a combination of unfortunate circumstances has blocked the development of a generally accepted scientific language. After one century, psychologists still do not agree on how to describe, explain, and predict psychological phenomena. The reasons for this are complex and much discussed and will not be treated in any detail here. However, by way of summary, it is likely that many of the difficulties stem from an incompatibility between some features of a scientific ideal inherited from the older physical sciences and the particular characteristics of psychological phenomena. Two oppositions are particularly important: the physical sciences strive to be *objective,* whereas psychological phenomena are *subjective,* and the physical sciences involve *empirical* study of hitherto *unknown* domains, whereas psychological phenomena are often *well known* and highly predictable in advance to ordinary people. These two oppositions will be briefly considered.

In line with their scientific ideal, research psychologists have tried to develop an objective and empirical science to deal with their subject matter. This approach to psychology has maintained itself over a century by producing a steady supply of objective data to be explained by causal theories. This has been possible because, unfortunately, one can always select or manufacture reliably observable objective characteristics of situations, behaviors, and behavior outcomes and formulate causal hypotheses about how these are related. Hence, the typical psychological study still relies on an objective description of the situation, the instructions, and the behavior of the participants. For example, pushing buttons or marking alternatives are popular and easy-to-score objective indices. The flaw in this approach is that there are no fixed relationships between objective features of situations and responses and their *meaning* for the persons involved. Any objective feature can have any meaning and, conversely, any meaning can be expressed through any objective feature. Hence, the typical specimen of contemporary psychological research manages to *look like* a study of causal relationships between objective events, while it *actually* depends on subtle interpretations of meanings in a complex context in order to maintain contact with what actually goes on psychologically, that is, *for* the participants.

Researchers know that the meanings of situations and behaviors cannot be directly observed, but have to be *understood*. However, in order to preserve the image of studying objective events, they usually take it for granted silently that situations are perceived in certain ways and that behaviors have certain meanings. By evading the problem of interpretation they also evade the fact that subjective events are *logically* rather than causally related. Seeing a red light does not *cause* a person to stop but is a *reason* for his or her stopping. The complex argumentation for the distinction between causes and reasons will not be repeated here. I will simply conclude that the notion of studying objective events, taken from physics, simply does not fit psychology. Objective events occur independently of persons, whereas psychological events occur *for* persons. Research psychologists are caught in an enduring conflict between their program of observing causal relationships between objective events and a dim and uneasy realization that they are actually dealing with and trying to understand logically interrelated meanings. After all, psychology is not about the pushing of buttons as a physical event, but about the meaning of this movement for the person, which, again, depends on how the situation and the instructions are understood, and so on.

The preceding means that psychologists have not been able to make a clear decision about the *ontological* status of their subject matter. Is scientific psychology the study of phenomena which exist independently of persons, that is, *objectively*, or is it the study of phenomena which exist *for* persons, that is, *subjectively?* Objective psychology, dealing with externally defined situations and behaviors, is out of touch with what exists for people simply because, as was already pointed out, there are no stable bridges between the objective and the subjective. Subjective psychology is concerned with situations and behaviors as they exist for persons, and, therefore, has to be concerned with the understanding of meanings.

The persistent confusion between these two alternatives is probably the main reason why a unitary scientific language in psychology has not yet developed. In the system to be presented in this book, psychology is consistently taken to be the study of what exists *for* persons. Another opposition is the conflict between the ideal of studying hitherto unknown domains empirically and the realization that psychological phenomena are in many ways well known and only need to be explicated. The received view implies that there are regularities which can become known only through painstaking observations of objective events under controlled conditions. Throughout the past century one has continued to collect masses of data in order to find these alleged "laws of psychology." The program has been able to maintain itself only because it has capitalized on a certain ambiguity in the encountered uncertainty. When one does not know in advance how someone is going to behave in a given situation, this may be attributed *either* to a lack of relevant concrete information about the person and the context *or* to a lack of knowledge of general psychological laws. Psychological researchers tend to focus on the latter alternative. Through the customary practice of studying unknown individuals (strangers) in highly contrived (strange) laboratory situations, much uncertainty is generated, and, hence, the use of empirical methods comes to appear natural and unavoidable. The contrived uncertainty in these laboratory situations is, falsely, attributed to a lack of knowledge of psychological laws, rather than to a simple lack of information about the persons, and, hence, the illusion of doing empirical research in unknown domains is maintained.

The prevalence of such highly artificial research settings makes it appear almost senseless to even question the premise that psychology is and must be an empirical science. Nevertheless, this is precisely what I am going to do. In my view, the uncertainty generated by the custom of studying "strangers in strange situations" (ten minutes with each undergraduate student in the laboratory) stems, not from a lack of knowledge of "laws," but simply from a failure to gather the necessary information about the individual persons involved, including their exact understanding of the situation. When all relevant information has been obtained, behavior tends to be perfectly predictable and explainable. The illusion that one is looking for hitherto unknown empirical laws is maintained through refraining from gathering the necessary antecedent information. In contradistinction to the above research strategy of psychologists, a layperson who is asked to predict another person's behavior in a given situation will naturally try to obtain the information necessary for doing so. This will include trying to find out what the person wants, what options he or she sees, how the situation is perceived, what remote consequences and what norms are taken to be relevant, and so on. It should be emphasized that laypersons typically *know* what kind of information to look for, and that this knowledge is embedded in the natural language and the nonverbal norms of the surrounding culture.

In the present work, I will follow the strategy of the layperson rather than that of the traditional research psychologist. I will present parts of a conceptual system, extracted from ordinary language, which permit one to predict behavior, given sufficient information about antecedent conditions. The system specifies what sort of information is needed and shows the extent to which psychology is not empirical.

Consider for a moment the task of formulating a systematic explication of the common-sense psychology which enables one to describe, explain, and predict behavior in everyday life. The essentials of this psychology emerge as answers to the simple question, *"what do you need to know in order to predict a person's behavior at a given time"?* In order to analyze what is involved in this question in a generally applicable way, it is important to select a reference situation which is sufficiently complex to eliminate too simplistic conceptualizations. For example, one should consider verbal rather than nonverbal behavior and complex rather than elementary tasks. The following prototype situation may be used to demonstrate what must be required of any adequate psychological conceptual framework: *a psychologist (P) is studying a person (A) who is describing, explaining, and predicting the behavior of another person (B). The task of P is to describe, explain, and predict what A is doing.* The subsequent discussion presupposes that this kind of situation is accepted as belonging to the subject matter of psychology, and that the tasks outlined are taken to be legitimate concerns of psychologists.

The first point to be made is that, since *P*'s task is to describe, explain, and predict *what A* is doing, the latter must be specified. But diagnosing *what A* is doing cannot be done within an objective, that is, behavioristic, frame of reference. The sounds *A* is emitting have a meaning *for A*, namely as being descriptions, explanations, and predictions of *B*'s behavior. This meaning defines *what A* is doing. The task of *P* must, accordingly, be to describe what is going on *for A*. *P* cannot merely *observe A*'s behavior, but must understand what it *means*. This kind of analysis also necessitates the introduction of concepts such as *lying, pretending,* and *deceiving,* which are hard to define behaviorally.

A second point, not generally recognized by psychologists, is that regularities in data need not necessarily be empirical, that is, need not be knowable only through experience. Suppose that A describes B as being "surprised." P may then predict that A will answer "yes" to the question "Do you think that B has experienced something that B had not expected?", and also that A will predict that B too will answer "yes" to that same question. These predictions of P will tend to be verified, but the regularities involved cannot be regarded as reflecting empirical psychological laws. This is so because they are not arrived at through experience, but are necessary consequences of correct use of language. *If* a person is surprised, *then* it follows with logical necessity that this person must have experienced something which he or she had not expected. This is exactly analogous to saying that *if* the sum of two angles in a triangle is equal to 90°, *then* the remaining angle must be equal to 90°. Hence, some findings are not empirical, but follow necessarily from the concepts implicit in the given descriptions. If, for example, B had not answered "yes," the conclusion would have been, not a weakening of a hypothetical empirical law, but that B was not, after all, surprised, *or* that he or she was not honest.

The same kind of analysis applies, for example, to the well-worn case about bachelors. The finding that all bachelors are in fact unmarried males cannot be said to be empirical. If the data appear to include a few bachelors who are females, we have to conclude either that these are, after all, not bachelors, or that they are not females. The descriptive proposition "this person is a bachelor and a female" is simply an incorrect and unacceptable description of the world in standard English. Hence, the link between being a bachelor and being an unmarried male is not an empirical finding and requires no empirical research.

Finally, a similar analysis may be applied to cases of nonverbal behavior such as the following: a person asks a uniformed attendant whether a museum is open and the attendant *shakes his head*. It may, then, be predicted that the person will not try to enter the museum. The subsequent observation that the person does not try to enter the museum is not empirical since it follows from the known meaning of the original question and the head shaking. If the person, after all, tries to enter, we may interpret it as indicating that he or she did not see the guard's shaking of his head, or pretends not to see it, and so on. In general, predictions which can be made solely on the basis of one's mastery of a language and membership in a given culture may be characterized as a priori since they neither require empirical support nor are affected by a lack of such support. There are normatively correct and normatively incorrect ways of speaking and of behaving nonverbally, and knowledge of these allows one to make extensive and generally correct predictions. When the predictions are falsified, this does not weaken any empirical hypothesis, but simply means that the assumed antecedent conditions had not been established. The present work contains only nonempirical propositions, presumably acceptable to every reader.

The given complex model example, involving three persons and descriptions, explanations and predictions, may also lead one to wonder about the exact relationship between the language of the psychologist and the language of the persons studied. When the psychologist wants to describe *what* another person is saying, it is impossible to do this without either repeating or rephrasing what is said. But rephrasing it means finding an exactly synonymous formulation, which is generally hard and risky. Hence, the safest way is to *repeat* what is heard. If *A* says, "I think *B* is surprised," *P* can only report, "*A* said, 'I think *B* is surprised'." Similarly, *P* can only repeat *A*'s explanations and predictions. For example, if *A* says, "I think *B* was surprised because it started to rain," *P* can explain *A*'s explanation only through referring to the same reasons that *A* would give. Suppose that *A* explains his or her own explanation by saying, "I think that is the correct explanation because *B* became surprised at the very moment it started to rain, and I remember *B* referring to the weather forecast as involving zero-expected rainfall." In this case, *P* will have to explain *A*'s explanation of *B*'s surprise by referring to the same circumstances that *A* referred to in his or her explanation. This means that *P*'s descriptive, explanatory, and predictive psychological language becomes *identical* to the corresponding natural language used by the persons studied, in this case *A*. The advantage of this identity both in form and meaning is that *P* can explain and predict much of what *A* will say and do in other situations, too. In general, then, the preceding means that scientific psychological language must be identical to the language of the persons studied. But how can this be reconciled with the usual requirements of a scientific language, notably precision and simplicity? Ordinary language has a very rich vocabulary with many partly synonymous terms and is characterized by an extremely high degree of context dependence. Typically, the meaning of words and sentences varies very much with the actual context, and this variability can hardly be reduced to any simple rules. How, then, can ordinary language be used in scientific psychology?

My answer to this question goes as follows. I believe that, even though ordinary words have very variable meanings, they also have a stable core meaning, and many partly overlapping words may also refer to the same core meaning. It appears to me that one may, to a considerable extent, define central concepts in ways which are acceptable and noncontroversial to both laypeople and psychologists as long as they are speakers of the given language and members of the given culture. This network of core concepts may then be used to derive propositions which are also acceptable to all speakers of the language and members of the culture, given plausible definitions of the concepts involved. In summary, it may be possible to explicate a skeleton system of important concepts underlying the complex surface of an ordinary language. In order to be acceptable for scientific purposes, this explicated system must have two important characteristics. One is that the derivations of its propositions should be stringent, and the other is that the formulation of its concepts and axioms should be acceptable to everyone speaking the language and being a member of the culture. The formulation of such a system can only approximate some of the psychologically relevant features of ordinary language and must necessarily ignore others. However, one may envisage successively more complex scientific languages, including an ever higher number of psychologically important distinctions.

Implicit in the above is a concept of common sense and a concept of a valid explication of common sense. By *the common sense of culture C* is meant here *the set of all implications taken for granted by all members of C.* This concept of common sense refers to consensual agreement on what follows from what. However, the agreement is normally only tacit, that is, people are not aware of what they take for granted. In order to use commonsense knowledge, it must be explicated. *A proposition stating an implication is a valid explication of psychological common sense to the extent that the members of the culture involved agree that the proposition is necessarily correct and that its negation is necessarily incorrect.* The system to be presented in this book is intended to consist exclusively of valid explications of psychological common sense.

The strongest defense for the project engaged in here lies in the intuitive recognition, shared by everyone, of the considerable *constraints* involved in ordinary language and in the nonverbal behavior patterns of a culture. There are so many things which cannot be said or done, so many possible sentences and combinations of acts which do *not* make sense. The, frequently successful, explanations and predictions of everyday life capitalize on these constraints. A science of psychology must utilize whatever order may exist in its subject matter and, hence, must begin by exploiting the highly successful everyday commonsense psychology.

This book reports the outcome of an effort to do this. The outcome should be judged on its own merits and no further metatheoretical justification will be presented here. The reader who is interested in more extensive discussions of the background for the present approach is referred to Appendix 3 for a list of references and also for a list of critiques of the present type of approach.

In my view, the predictive and explanatory power of the nonempirical system to be presented far exceeds that of any existing psychological theory. As I see it, this system may replace many preceding empirical psychological theories and reflects an alternative and more adequate view of psychology. According to this, psychology is the study of the culturally created order in human behavior, and this is the only order to be found in this domain, besides the biological constraints within which each individual functions. The culturally created order is taken for granted unreflectively by every speaker of the given language and member of the given culture and, hence, only needs to be explicated. This explication may sometimes be difficult, but it still involves exploration of what is already tacitly known, rather than of something previously unknown. This fundamentally redefines the task for psychological research.

1 Being Aware and Active

Note 1.0.0 In this work, P and Q designate persons; $A_1, A_2, \ldots$ designate activities as they exist for the actor; $B_1, B_2, \ldots$ designate beliefs; $C_1, C_2, \ldots$ designate contexts; $F_1, F_2, \ldots$ designate feelings; $O_1, O_2, \ldots$ designate objects of awareness; $t_1, t_2, \ldots$ designate times or time intervals; $W_1, W_2, \ldots$ designate wants.

1.1 Awareness

Definition 1.1.0 **"P is aware of O"= df "O exists for P."**

Note 1.1.1 The mode of existing *for* someone defines a domain of investigation clearly different from that of natural science which studies events taken to exist *independently* of the observer. The distinction dependence/independence of an observer should not be confused with the *influence* of the observer and of instruments on the phenomena. In microphysics, what is observed is radically influenced by the measuring instruments, and in psychology by the presence vs. absence of an observer. However, the dependence implied by Definition 1.1.0 is *definitional*. Something cannot be said to exist *for* someone, if there is no one *for* whom it exists. Phenomena which exist independently of a person can be said to exist even if that person no longer exists.

Note 1.1.2 The *"O"* in *"O exists for P"* should not be confused with an object existing independently of *P*, either existing through consensus (social object) or independently of consensus (material object). The object that exists for *P* may be *correlated* with a social object or with a material object. If *P* always behaves according to the prevalent moral code in *P*'s society, it may be inferred that the moral code as it exists *for P* appears to be highly correlated with the moral code as defined through consensus. Similarly, if *P*'s eyes follow the movements of a stick that is moved in front of *P*, it may be inferred that *for P* there exists something whose movements correspond closely to those of the material stick. In everyday life, one may frequently ignore the distinctions between the material, the social, and the subjective because of the high correlations between them. In this work, whose topic is conceptual analysis, the distinctions are important.

Note 1.1.3 To say that *P* is not aware of *O,* means that *O* does not exist for *P.*

Note 1.1.4 For some purposes, an enriched terminology of objects may be needed. Objects of awareness could continue to be represented as "*O,*" social objects could be symbolized as *O$_s$,*" and material objects as "*O$_m$.*" Only one necessary link exists between these. If something is a social object, then it must correspond to an object of awareness of many persons. Otherwise, an object of awareness, a social object, or a material object, may or may not correspond to a member of one or both of the two other categories.

Definition 1.1.5 **"*P* is conscious"** = df **"*P* is in a state in which he or she can become aware of something."**

Corollary 1.1.6 **If *P* is aware of *O,* then *P* is conscious.** Proof: this follows directly from Definition 1.1.5.

Theorem 1.1.7 **If *P* is conscious, then *P* is aware of something.** Proof: this follows from Definition 1.1.5 and the assumption that there is always something one can be aware of.

Note 1.1.8 The fruitfulness of the dispositional concept of consciousness lies in that if *P* is aware of something, then *P* can usually become aware of other things normally accessible to *P*'s awareness and, conversely, if *P* does not become aware of anything normally accessible to *P*'s awareness, then *P* may be expected not to become aware of other things normally accessible to *P*'s awareness. The trivial illustration of this is that if *P* responds normally to one ordinary-type stimulation, then *P* is expected to respond normally to other ordinary-type stimulations, and conversely for the negative case.

Note 1.1.9 One may distinguish between *degrees* of consciousness, from being fully unconscious to being fully conscious. In what follows, these distinctions are not considered, and all persons are simply taken to be fully conscious.

1.2 Activity

Definition 1.2.0 **"*P* acts"** = df **"*P* does something in order to achieve a goal, taking into account what he or she is aware of and takes to be relevant for the project of achieving that goal."**

Note 1.2.1 One may distinguish between *overt behavior* through which the person brings about changes in the social and/or the material world, and *co-*

vert behavior through which the person brings about changes in the subjective world only (perceiving, imagining, dreaming, thinking, recollecting, and so on). Covert behavior is the construction and reconstruction of objects of awareness. The essential identity of overt and covert activity, both confirming to the structural Definition 1.2.0, is seen in the case of a blind or blindfolded person who is asked to identify an object. The handmovements are, at the same time, overt behavior, turning the object around and touching it on all sides, and covert behavior, gathering information and constructing an object of awareness.

Corollary 1.2.2 **If *P* does something not in order to achieve a goal, then what *P* does is not an act.** Proof: this follows directly from Definition 1.2.0.

Note 1.2.3 The preceding corollary emphasizes the intentional nature of acting and points out that what is not goal directed falls outside the category of acting used here.

Definition 1.2.4 **"*P* acts overtly"** = df **"*P* does something which brings about changes in the social and/or material world."**

Definition 1.2.5 **"*P* acts covertly"** = df **"*P* does something which brings about changes in the subjective world (constructing and reconstructing objects of awareness)."**

Note 1.2.6 Overt activity informed by awareness is a concept very different from physical movement. The same physical movement may involve different acts, and the same act may involve different physical movements. Also, the physical movement of a person may not involve acting at all. Examples of this would be slipping on a banana peel or twitching from an electric shock. Finally, an overt act may involve no physical movement at all and yet may lead to social and/or material consequences. It may simply consist in *refraining* from doing something or being *silent* about something. Here, awareness of an *alternative* is presupposed. Also, overt activity, as seen by the actor, may be different from the socially defined activity of that same person. A person may believe that he or she has conveyed sympathy to someone, whereas the consensual opinion is that he or she has behaved in a rejecting manner. A person may perform an overt act, that is, an act with social and/or material consequences, without anyone recognizing it. Conversely, a person may believe he or she has done nothing overtly, while others agree that he or she has carried out a definite act. Finally, a person may believe he or she has acted overtly, whereas, in fact, the act was only covert.

Axiom 1.2.7 **A conscious person is continuously acting.**

Note 1.2.8 This axiom means that being conscious involves unceasing activity. It also means that, even if no discernible overt activity occurs, there is always covert activity.

Definition 1.2.9 **"P takes the presence vs. absence of O_1 to be relevant for the project of achieving O_2" = df "P takes the presence vs. absence of O_1 to indicate a possible difference in the likelihood of achieving O_2, in at least one context and/or for at least one combination of acts."**

Note 1.2.10 Definition 1.2.9 states that something is taken to be relevant for a project if, and only if, its presence vs. absence is taken to make for a possible difference in the likelihood of success of at least one way of trying to achieve the goal, and/or in at least one situation.

Note 1.2.11 In what follows, the single term "act" will be used to refer both to overt and covert action in order to simplify the propositions. However, the reader is reminded that although the terminology is a little awkward and departs from ordinary usage of the terms, the simplification is well justified. Just as persons act overtly to achieve socially and/or materially defined goals, they act covertly to achieve the goal of correct understanding, see below.

Note 1.2.12 The delimitation of an act must always involve a specification of for whom the act is taken to exist. This may be the actor and/or some other person or persons. An act does not exist "objectively," that is, independently of how persons view it.

Definition 1.2.13 **"P takes O into account in his or her acts" = df "Changes in O directly or indirectly make a difference in the way P acts."**

Note 1.2.14 O_1 makes an *indirect* difference, for example, when a change in O_1 makes a difference, not directly in how P acts, but in *how* a change in O_2, if it were to occur, would make a difference in how P acts.

Corollary 1.2.15 **If P is aware of O_1, if P takes O_1 to be relevant for the project of achieving O_2, and if P performs an act directed at achieving O_2, then P takes O_1 into account in performing that act.** Proof: according to Definition 1.2.0, "P acts" is equivalent to "P does something in order to achieve a goal, taking into account what he or she is aware of and takes to be relevant for the project of achieving that goal." But, since P is acting toward achieving O_2, and is aware of O_1 and takes O_1 to be relevant for achieving O_2, it follows that P will take O_1 into account.

Theorem 1.2.16 **If a change in O makes for a difference in P's acting in C at t, then P is aware of O in C at t, and takes O to be relevant for P's project at hand.** Proof: according to Definition 1.2.13, if a change in O makes for a difference in P's acting, then P takes O into account in his or her acting. But, according to Definition 1.2.0, if P acts and takes O into account in his or her acting, then P must be aware of O and take O to be relevant for P's project at hand.

1.3 Reflectivity

Definition 1.3.0   *"P is reflectively aware of O"*= df *"P is aware that* **he or she is aware of** *O."*

Definition 1.3.1   *"P is unreflectively aware of O"*= df *"P is aware of O, but P is not reflectively aware of O."*

Note 1.3.2   The definitions of "reflective" and "unreflective awareness" are exhaustive and mutually exclusive. If *P* is aware of *O,* then *P* is either reflectively or unreflectively aware of *O,* but not both. In reality, one may probably observe intermediate or mixed cases, too.

Note 1.3.3   Reflective awareness is a second-order awareness of the person's first-order awareness. It involves a differentiation between the fact *that* one is aware of something, and *what* one is aware *of.* This distinction is not involved in unreflective awareness. Reflective awareness also involves a distinction between the content of one's awareness and reality, which means a recognition of subjectivity and the possibility of error. Unreflective awareness does not recognize subjectivity. When awareness is reflective, at least four possible levels may be involved: (a) awareness that one's awareness is reflective; (b) reflective awareness; (c) awareness of something; and (d) awareness that one's awareness of something may be true or false or more or less probable. Example: *P* looks at a stick half immersed in water and may produce the following four statements: (a) "I am aware that my awareness at this moment is reflective"; (b) "I am aware that I am aware of the stick"; (c) "there is a stick and it looks broken"; (d) "I am aware that this is only apparent and that the real stick is unbroken"

Axiom 1.3.4   **A person can describe that of which he or she is reflectively aware and only that.**

Note 1.3.5   Reflective awareness is a direct and necessary consequence of the acquisition of language. In other words, by learning to describe what they are aware of, persons, by definition, acquire reflective awareness.

Corollary 1.3.6   **If P is reflectively aware of O, then P can describe O.** Proof: this follows directly from Axiom 1.3.4.

Corollary 1.3.7   **If P can describe O, then P is reflectively aware of O.** Proof: this follows directly from Axiom 1.3.4.

Note 1.3.8   In practice, Corollary 1.3.7 is often used to determine whether or not there is reflective awareness of something. If there are no signs of reflective awareness, the possible existence of unreflective awareness of *O* may be established through observing if the person consistently acts *as if O* were the case. In the case of deceit, the observation that *P* acts as if *O* were the case, while denying all knowledge of *O,* may also serve as incriminating evidence.

11

Note 1.3.9 One may, in principle, distinguish between at least three main categories of unreflective awareness. First, *P* may be only unreflectively aware of *O* simply because there has been no occasion for *P* to reflect upon that awareness. In this case, it may be sufficient to draw *P*'s attention to his or her awareness of *O* in order to get reflective awareness on *P*'s part. Secondly, it may be difficult for *P* to become reflectively aware of *O*, because of its complexity and/or its incommensurability with available linguistic categories. In the former case, prolonged training may be necessary, and, in the latter case, training to become reflectively aware may be impossible. In general, many motor performances and social performances may be so complex and require such subtle and rapid adjustments that reflection cannot do justice to them and may even have a destructive effect. A third category of unreflective awareness refers to when *P*, unreflectively, wants *not* to become reflectively aware of *O*, although this would be possible, because this is, unreflectively, believed to be intolerably painful. Example: a person is attracted to another person of the same sex. To become reflectively aware of this would be very frightening and, hence, the attraction remains unreflective and is only revealed indirectly in aspects of the person's behavior.

Definition 1.3.10 **"*P* acts reflectively" = df "*P* acts and *P* is aware that he or she acts in this way and why he or she does so."**

Corollary 1.3.11 **If *P* acts reflectively, then *P* is aware of that the act is directed at a certain goal and that he or she is aware of certain things and takes them into account because they are taken to be relevant for the project of achieving the goal.** Proof: this follows directly from the definitions of an act (1.2.0) and of a reflective act (1.3.10).

Note 1.3.12 Probably no purely reflective act has ever occurred. One always takes many more things for granted than one can be reflectively aware of. However, one may distinguish between more or less reflective acts.

Definition 1.3.13 **"*P* acts unreflectively" = df "*P* acts, but is not aware that he or she acts in this way and is not aware of why he or she does so."**

Corollary 1.3.14 **If *P* acts unreflectively, then *P* is not aware that the act is directed at a certain goal and that he or she is aware of certain things and takes them into account because they are taken to be relevant for the project of achieving the goal.** Proof: this follows directly from the definitions of an act (1.2.0) and an unreflective act (1.3.13).

Note 1.3.15 The difficulty of the idea of unreflective acting stems from the fact that we can only talk about what we are reflectively aware of. Every time we try to grasp what we may be doing unreflectively, we focus on it reflectively, and it is no longer unreflective. On the other hand, what we do unreflectively and do *not* contemplate reflectively, remains undiscovered and undescribed. We live with the conviction that we know what we are doing, or at least, can know it, if need be. The recognition of the limitations of reflective awareness therefore often comes from contemplating the activity of *others*. Sometimes, we also come across traces of our own activity which show that we must have done something without being aware that we were doing it. "The piece of soap is in the refrigerator, so I must have put it there, while thinking of something else."

Theorem 1.3.16 **Talking is acting reflectively.** Proof: according to Axiom 1.3.4, *P* can describe that of which *P* is reflectively aware and only that. But description of talk involves simple repetition of that talk. Hence, talking can always be described by the talker. It follows from this and Axiom 1.3.4 that talking involves reflective awareness and, hence, according to Definition 1.3.10, is acting reflectively.

Theorem 1.3.17 **Listening to talk involves reflective awareness.** Proof: according to Axiom 1.3.4, *P* can describe that of which *P* is reflectively aware and only that. But description of talk involves simple repetition of that talk. Hence, talking can always be described by the listener. It follows from this and Axiom 1.3.4 that listening to talk involves reflective awareness.

Note 1.3.18 A person who says *"X"* can always, immediately afterwards, say, "I said *'X'*," and talk about that. Listening to oneself and listening to others both involve reflective awareness. Axiom 1.3.4 and Theorems 1.3.16 and 1.3.17 are quite distinct in their content. Axiom 1.3.4 has to do with what one talks *about,* Theorem 1.3.16 has to do with the act of talking itself, and Theorem 1.3.17 has to do with listening to talking. In talking, one is reflectively aware both of what one is talking about and of the fact that one is talking about it. It follows from the preceding that "talking in one's sleep" cannot be said to be an instance of talking proper.

Note 1.3.19 Theorem 1.3.16 states that if one is talking, one is acting reflectively. However, it does not state that if one is acting reflectively one is talking. Hence, talking is a subclass of reflective acting. Similarly, Theorem 1.3.17 states that if one is listening to talk one is reflectively aware. However, it does not state that if one is reflectively aware, one is listening to talk. Hence, listening to talk is a subclass of reflective awareness.

Note 1.3.20 Unreflective awareness has belief-character in the sense that what is apprehended always *refers to* something. Hence, it is always subject to possible error. On the other hand, *P*'s reflective awareness is not fallible. While *P* may be mistaken about seeing an oasis. *P* may not be mistaken in being aware *that* he or she is seeing an oasis. This may be formally expressed as follows:

13

Axiom 1.3.21 **Reflective awareness defines an object of awareness.**

Note 1.3.22 A person may lie in reporting an experience, but when the person is honest and regards his or her own report as adequate, this *defines* what the person is aware of.

Corollary 1.3.23 **If *P* in *C* at *t* is reflectively aware of *O*, then *P*'s description of *O* is correct, to the extent that *P* regards it as correct.** Proof: according to Axiom 1.3.21 reflective awareness defines an object of awareness. Therefore, *P*'s reflective awareness defines *O*, that is, *O* is what *P* is aware of that *P* is aware of. If *P* describes what he or she is aware of, then he or she describes *O*. If the description is regarded by *P* as correct, then it correctly describes *O*.

Note 1.3.24 The logic of this is intricate. First, by assuming that *P* regards the description as correct, ordinary deceit is ruled out. Secondly, although *P* regards the description as correct, this may not accord with other persons' use of the given language. What is asserted is that if *P* regards the description as adequate, then it is a correct description as far as *P*'s use of language is concerned. Since *O* exists for *P*, there is, in principle, no way for others to evaluate the relation between *O* and *P*'s description of *O*.

Note 1.3.25 Suppose that *P* describes herself as "unable to be angry," and that this is a description that *P* regards as correct. The fact that this is a correct description of *P*'s reflective experience of herself does not mean that it is, necessarily, a correct description of *P*. It may be that *P* has unreflective feelings of anger which may be inferred by others from *P*'s overt behavior.

1.4 Persons

Definition 1.4.0 **"A person" = df "One who can be reflectively aware."**

Note 1.4.1 This is a definition of a central term by reference to one necessary and sufficient criterion which has a long tradition in Western culture. The definition uses the form "can" because no one is reflectively aware all the time and in every respect.

Theorem 1.4.2 **If *P* can talk, then *P* is a person.** Proof: it follows from Corollary 1.3.7 that if *P* can talk about *O*, then *P* can be reflectively aware of *O*. But, according to Definition 1.4.0, if *P* can be reflectively aware, then *P* is a person, and, hence, the theorem follows.

Note 1.4.3 It has *not* been asserted that if *P* is a person, then *P* can talk. There are persons who cannot talk. However, if instead of talking one uses the criterion of "using a language," then it would be true that if *P* is a person, then *P* can use a language. This could, for example, be the sign language of the deaf mutes.

Note 1.4.4 Definition 1.4.0 serves to distinguish persons from animals. Animals too are aware and act, but they do not seem to be aware *that* they are aware and *that* they act. Even the artificial languages of chimpanzees do not seem to include the self-reflexive mode of talking *about* talking and talking *about* own behavior, which is embedded in human language.

Note 1.4.5 Persons are highly distinct entities just as organisms are. Although, normally, one person corresponds to one human organism, the phenomena of *multiple personalities* highlight the fact that an organism and a person are quite different concepts. Two or more persons can be clearly distinguished, even though they are manifested by the same organism. Human organisms have sometimes been kept alive, even when the corresponding person no longer existed.

Definition 1.4.6 **"Human psychology"** = df **"The study of persons."**

Note 1.4.7 The field of study includes not only the reflective, but also the unreflective awareness and acting of persons. As defined here, human psychology is a science of the mental, concerned with what exists *for* persons.

1.5 Unity of the Person

Axiom 1.5.0 **A person's awareness and acting tend to be completely integrated (unitary).**

Note 1.5.1 The integration means that everything taken to be relevant also tends to be taken into account in the construction of every object of awareness and every act. This can be expressed in the following two corollaries:

Corollary 1.5.2 **If *P* is aware of O_1 and O_2 and *P* takes O_2 to be relevant for the construction of O_1, then *P* will tend to take O_2 into account in construing O_1.** Proof: this follows directly from Axiom 1.5.0.

Corollary 1.5.3 **If *P* is aware of O_1 and O_2 and *P* takes O_2 to be relevant for how to act overtly relative to O_1, then *P* will tend to take O_2 into account in acting overtly relative to O_1.** Proof: this follows directly from Axiom 1.5.0.

Note 1.5.4 Obviously, neither organisms nor persons achieve perfect integration. Nevertheless, the most general statement that can be made is that there is a close approximation to this state. In everyday life, people tend to take Corollaries 1.5.2 and 1.5.3 for granted and use them to make inferences and predictions.

Definition 1.5.5 **"The context of an object of awareness or an act of P" $=$ df "The set of everything of which P is aware and which P takes to be relevant for construing the given object of awareness or for attaining the goal of the given act."**

Theorem 1.5.6 **The context of P's awareness of O, or of P's acting relative to O, consists of what P takes into account in his or her construing of O or his or her acting relative to O.** Proof: according to Definition 1.5.5, the context of an object of awareness or an act consists of everything the person is aware of and takes to be relevant. But, according to Corollary 1.2.15, if a person is aware of something and takes it to be relevant, then the person takes it into account. Hence, the theorem follows.

Note 1.5.7 The awareness and acting of persons is characterized by exceedingly complex contexts in which the parts tend to be mutually dependent. The determination of contexts is a major practical problem in psychology.

Note 1.5.8 There are three logically possible basic types of integration or contexts, all of which occur frequently. Let us use the following symbolism: O_1 and O_2 are two of P's objects of awareness, A_1 and A_2 are two of P's acts, $X \rightarrow Y$ means that Y is formed taking X into account, and $X \leftrightarrow Y$ means that X and Y are formed taking each other mutually into account. The three types may, then, be represented as follows:

    a. **Simultaneous**   b. **Planned, successive**   c. **Unplanned, successive**
       integration   **integration**   **integration**

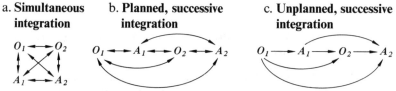

Note 1.5.9 In planned successive integration, each object of awareness and each act is construed in a context of earlier and of planned future events. Unplanned successive integration involves only accumulating memories of past events and no expectancies of future events. In all three cases O_1, A_1, and O_2 form part of the context of A_2, in case c. A_2 is not part of the context of O_2, and so on.

1.6 Past, Present, and Future

Note 1.6.0 It is apparent from the diagrams presented above that contexts may include both past, present, and future objects of awareness and acts. The appropriate terms for characterizing the person's awareness and activity relative to the temporal dimension are defined below ($C =$ context).

Definition 1.6.1   *"P* in *C$_2$* at *t$_2$* reflectively remembers *O* in *C$_1$* at *t$_1$"* = df *"P* in *C$_2$* at *t$_2$* is aware that he or she was aware of *O* in *C$_1$* at *t$_1$."*

Note 1.6.2   Reflective remembering implies that *P* can talk about the past. This can be formally expressed as follows:

Theorem 1.6.3   **If *P* in *C$_2$* at *t$_2$* reflectively remembers *O* in *C$_1$* at *t$_1$*, then *P* in *C$_2$* at *t$_2$* can talk about *O* in *C$_1$* at *t$_1$*.** Proof: according to Definition 1.6.1, if *P* reflectively remembers *O* in *C$_1$* at *t$_1$*, then *P* is aware that he or she was aware of *O* in *C$_1$* at *t$_1$*. But, if *P* is aware that he or she was aware of *O* in *C$_1$* at *t$_1$*, then, according to Definition 1.3.0, *P* is reflectively aware of *O* in *C$_1$* at *t$_1$*. From this and Axiom 1.3.4 it follows that *P* in *C$_2$* at *t$_2$* can talk about *O* in *C$_1$* at *t$_1$*.

Definition 1.6.4   *"P* in *C$_2$* at *t$_2$* unreflectively remembers *O* in *C$_1$* at *t$_1$"* = df *"P* in *C$_2$* at *t$_2$* is aware of at least one consequence of *O* having occurred in *C$_1$* at *t$_1$*, but is not aware that he or she is aware of this."*

Note 1.6.5   Unreflective remembering is only revealed in that *P* acts *as if O* had taken place, in other words, taking for granted that *O* has taken place. Activity dependent on such remembering can only be recognized if the awareness that *O* has taken place has some distinctive consequences for action in a later situation.

Definition 1.6.6   *"P* in *C$_2$* at *t$_2$* has forgotten *O* in *C$_1$* at *t$_1$* at the reflective level"* = df *"P* was aware of *O* in *C$_1$* at *t$_1$*, but *P* in *C$_2$* at *t$_2$* is not aware that he or she was aware of *O* in *C$_1$* at *t$_1$."*

Note 1.6.7   Forgetting is an exception to the almost complete integration postulated by Axiom 1.5.0. However, it should be emphasized that in real life remembering of what is relevant is the rule and forgetting is the exception. Extensive breakdown of ability to remember incapacitates a person.

Note 1.6.8   Forgetting at the reflective level does not imply that there is also forgetting at the unreflective level. This may or may not be the case.

Definition 1.6.9   *"P* in *C$_2$* at *t$_2$* has forgotten *O* in *C$_1$* at *t$_1$* at the unreflective level"* = df *"P* was aware of *O* in *C$_1$* at *t$_1$*, but *P* in *C$_2$* at *t$_2$* is not aware of any consequences of *O* having occurred in *C$_1$* at *t$_1$*.

Note 1.6.10   Forgetting at the unreflective level means that *P* acts *as if O* had not taken place, in other words, *P* acts taking for granted that *O* has not occurred. Forgetting at the unreflective level implies forgetting at the reflective level, too, since if there is no awareness, there can be no awareness that there is awareness.

Note 1.6.11   That *O* is forgotten at the reflective, or even at the unreflective level, does not mean that *O* cannot be remembered again, at a later time under some other circumstances.

17

Definition 1.6.12   *"P* in *C* at *t* reflectively perceives *O"* = df *P* in *C* at *t* is aware that he or she is aware of *O."*

Note 1.6.13   Reflective perception means that *P* can talk about present events. Formally, this is expressed as follows:

Theorem 1.6.14   **If *P* in *C* at *t* reflectively perceives *O*, then *P* in *C* at *t* can talk about *O*.** Proof: according to Definition 1.6.12, if *P* reflectively perceives *O*, then *P* is aware that he or she is aware of *O*. But, according to Definition 1.3.0, this means that *P* is reflectively aware of *O*. It then follows from Axiom 1.3.4 that *P* can talk about *O*.

Definition 1.6.15   *"P* in *C* at *t* unreflectively perceives *O"* = df *"P* in *C* at *t* is aware of *O*, but is not aware that he or she is aware of *O."*

Note 1.6.16   Unreflective perception is only revealed in that *P* acts *as if* an event is taking place. *P* cannot talk about this.

Theorem 1.6.17   **If *P* in *C* at *t* unreflectively perceives *O*, then *P* in *C* at *t* cannot talk about *O*.** Proof: according to Definition 1.6.15, if *P* unreflectively perceives *O*, then *P* is not aware that he or she is aware of *O*. But, according to Definition 1.6.15, this means that *P* is unreflectively aware of *O*. It then follows from Axiom 1.3.4 that *P* cannot talk about *O*.

Definition 1.6.18   *"P* in C_1 at t_1 reflectively expects *O* in C_2 at t_2"* = df *"P* in C_1 at t_1 is aware that he or she expects *O* in C_2 at t_2."*

Note 1.6.19   Reflective expectancy means that one can talk about the future. Formally this is expressed as follows:

Theorem 1.6.20   **If *P* in C_1 at t_1 reflectively expects *O* in C_2 at t_2, then *P* in C_1 at t_1 can talk about *O* in C_2 at t_2.** Proof: according to Definition 1.6.18, if *P* in C_1 at t_1 reflectively expects *O* in C_2 at t_2, then *P* in C_1 at t_1 is aware that he or she expects *O* in C_2 at t_2. But, according to Definition 1.3.0, this means that *P* is reflectively aware of expecting *O* in C_2 at t_2. It follows from this, according to Axiom 1.3.4, that *P* can talk about *O* in C_2 at t_2.

Definition 1.6.21   *"P* in C_1 at t_1 unreflectively expects *O* in C_2 at t_2"* = df *"P* expects *O* in C_2 at t_2, but is not aware of this."*

Note 1.6.22   Unreflective expectancy cannot be talked about. This is formally proved as follows:

Theorem 1.6.23   **If *P* in C_1 at t_1 unreflectively expects *O* in C_2 at t_2, then *P* in C_1 at t_1 cannot talk about expecting *O* in C_2 at t_2.** Proof: according to Definition 1.6.21, if *P* in C_1 at t_1 unreflectively expects *O* in C_2 at t_2, then *P* in C_1 at t_1 is not aware that he or she expects *O* in C_2 at t_2. But, according to Definition 1.3.1, this means that *P* in C_1 at t_1 is only unreflectively aware of expecting *O* in C_2 at t_2. It follows from this and Axiom 1.3.4 that *P* in C_1 at t_1 cannat talk about expecting *O* in C_2 at t_2.

Note 1.6.24 Unreflective expectancy is only revealed in that P acts *as if O is* going to take place, or, in other words, taking for granted that O is going to take place. This can only be diagnosed if there are some distinctive consequences for P's acting in C_1 at t_1.

Note 1.6.25 Differentiation between reference to the past, the present, and the future occurs only at the level of reflective awareness. Consider the case of a small child who cannot talk, withdrawing its hand from the stove, short of touching it. This act refers both to the past, when the child was burned, to the present expectancy, and to the future prospect of being burned again. In automatic, unreflective acts there is no *separate* reference to the past, the present, or the future.

Summary

When a person is aware of something, that thing exists *for* the person. To act is to try to achieve a goal, taking into account what is taken to be relevant for achieving that goal. Overt action is to try to bring about changes in the social and/or material world. Covert activity is to try to construe objects of awareness. "Human psychology" is defined as the study of persons, and "a person" is defined as one who can be reflectively aware and act reflectively. "Reflective awareness" is being aware *that* one is aware of something. Reflective awareness and talking are closely linked. One can talk about that of which one is reflectively aware and only that. Only persons can talk. "Unreflective awareness" is to take something for granted. The context of an awareness or an act is everything of which the person is aware that is taken to be relevant for the given awareness or act. Remembering, forgetting, perceiving, and expecting can all be both reflective and unreflective.

2 Wanting and Believing

Note 2.0.0 Two main determinants of what a person is aware of and does are his or her *wants* and *beliefs*. If **P** *wants* a cab, then **P** looks for a cab. If **P** *believes* that cabs are yellow and are most frequent on main streets, then **P** walks to such a street and pays attention to whether or not an approaching car is yellow, and so on.

2.1 Wants

Definition 2.1.0 **"P in C at t wants X"= df "P in C at t believes that X is not the case and P would like it to be the case, or P in C at t believes that X is the case and P would like it to continue to be the case."**

Note 2.1.1 Since anything may be inserted for *"X,"* this definition covers every conceivable type of want, including both wants to achieve and to maintain positive goals and wants to avoid or to escape negative goals. In all cases, wanting involves a direction towards something not yet realized.

Theorem 2.1.2 **A conscious person continuously wants something.** Proof: according to Axiom 1.2.7, a conscious person is continuously acting. But, according to Definition 1.2.0, acting involves doing something in order to achieve a goal and, hence, involves wanting. By this, the theorem is proved.

Definition 2.1.3 **"P in C at t is reflectively aware of that he or she wants X"= df "P in C at t is aware that he or she believes that X is not the case and would like it to be the case, or P in C at t is aware of that he or she believes that X is the case and would like it to continue to be the case."**

Corollary 2.1.4 **If P in C at t is reflectively aware that he or she wants X, then P in C at t can describe and talk about that want.** Proof: this follows directly from Definition 2.1.3 and Axiom 1.3.4.

Corollary 2.1.5 **If P in C at t can describe and talk about his or her want of X, then P in C at t is reflectively aware of that want.** Proof: this follows directly from Definition 2.1.3 and Axiom 1.3.4.

Note 2.1.6　*P* may very well be reflectively aware of his or her want of *X* and yet not actually describe it or talk about it. Only the *ability* to describe and talk about is involved here.

Definition 2.1.7　**"*P* in *C* at *t* is unreflectively aware that he or she wants *X*"** = df **"*P* in *C* at *t* is not aware that he or she would like *X* to be the case or that he or she would like *X* to continue to be the case."**

Note 2.1.8　*P* may well be reflectively aware of the presence or absence of *X* and still be only unreflectively aware of his or her want of *X*.

Corollary 2.1.9　**If *P* in *C* at *t* is only unreflectively aware that he or she wants *X*, then *P* in *C* at *t* cannot describe or talk about that want.** Proof: this follows directly from Definition 2.1.7 and Axiom 1.3.4.

Corollary 2.1.10　**If *P* in *C* at *t* cannot describe or talk about his or her want of *X*, then *P*'s want of *X* is unreflective.** Proof: this follows directly from Definition 2.1.7 and Axiom 1.3.4.

Note 2.1.11　The conjunction of Corollaries 2.1.4, 2.1.5, 2.1.9, and 2.1.10 is equivalent to Axiom 1.3.4 as it applies to the awareness of wants.

Note 2.1.12　Since it is *P* who wants, he or she cannot be unaware of the want. However, *P* may be only unreflectively aware of the want and, hence, unable to describe and talk about it.

Note 2.1.13　What persons want cannot be exhaustively categorized. It may range from getting rid of a minor itch to world peace. There is, in principle, no limit to what a person could want. However, there are things that all persons must want, simply because they are persons. These will be treated in Chapter 5.

Definition 2.1.14　**"*P*'s want *A* is stronger than *P*'s want *B*"** = df **"When *P*'s wants, *A* and *B*, are in conflict and all other factors are equal, *P* tries to act according to *A* and not according to *B*."**

Note 2.1.15　The preference for acting in accordance with *A* and not in accordance with *B*, when the wants are in conflict and all other factors are equal, describes a *criterion* of strength of a want. A criterion is valid by definition. It should be distinguished from a *symptom,* which is assumed to be correlated with an underlying state and which needs empirical validation.

Definition 2.1.16　**"Two wants are in conflict"** = df **"Acting according to one of the two wants is incompatible with acting according to the other."**

Note 2.1.17　What is acting according to a given want, for *P*, cannot be determined from knowledge of that want alone. One must also know *P*'s relevant beliefs. If *P* wants to visit a certain cinema and also wants to visit a certain restaurant, one cannot decide on the basis of this alone, which want *P* is acting in accordance with when taking a given bus. In order to make this decision, one has to know where *P* believes the cinema and the restaurant are situated and where *P* believes the bus is going. From the preceding it also follows that one cannot decide from knowing about *P*'s two wants whether they are in conflict or not. This only becomes clear when one, for example, comes to know that *P* believes that the cinema and the restaurant are situated so far apart that a visit to one of them precludes visiting the other one on the same trip.

Note 2.1.18 The following two corollaries are very frequently used in everyday life:

Corollary 2.1.19 **If *P*'s want *A* is stronger than *P*'s want *B*, then, when the wants are in conflict and all other factors are equal, *P* will try to act according to *A* and not according to *B*.** Proof: this follows directly from Definition 2.1.14.

Corollary 2.1.20 **If *P* tries to act according to want *A* and not according to want *B*, when the wants are in conflict and all other factors are equal, then *P*'s want *A* is stronger than *P*'s want *B*.** Proof: this follows directly from Definition 2.1.14.

Note 2.1.21 The term "factors" in Definition 2.1.14 and in Corollaries 2.1.19 and 2.1.20 refers to other wants and beliefs.

Corollary 2.1.22 **If *P*'s want *A* is stronger than *P*'s want *B* in *C* at *t*, and the wants are in conflict, and if, in *C* at *t*, *X* can be perceived either as *Y* or *not-Y*, or as *Z* or *not-Z*, and if *Y* or *not-Y* is taken by *P* to be relevant for the project of achieving the goal of want *A*, and *Z* or *not-Z* is taken by *P* to be relevant for the project of achieving the goal of want *B*, then *P* in *C* at *t* will perceive *X* as *Y* or *not-Y*, and not as *Z* or *not-Z*.** Proof: according to Definition 2.1.14, *P* in *C* at *t* will act according to want *A* and not according to want *B*. But, according to Definition 1.2.0, if *P* acts in order to achieve the goal of want *A*, then *P* will take into account what he or she takes to be relevant for the project of achieving that goal. Since *Y* and *not-Y* is taken by *P* to be relevant for the project of achieving the goal of want *A*, it follows that *P* will take into account, that is, perceive, *X* as *Y* or *not-Y* and not as *Z* or *not-Z*.

Note 2.1.23 In everyday life Corollary 2.1.22 is frequently applied in predicting how people will be perceptually selective according to their momentary dominant wants.

Note 2.1.24 It is implicit in the preceding that if two wants are *not* in conflict, their strengths will combine. In order to describe what is implied here, a definition of *"compatibility"* is needed:

Definition 2.1.25 **"Two wants are compatible" = df "Acting according to one of the two wants is compatible with acting according to the other."**

Note 2.1.26 Obviously two wants may be in conflict with respect to some ways of acting and compatible with respect to some other ways of acting.

Corollary 2.1.27 **If two wants, W_1 and W_2, are compatible with respect to act A in situation S at time t, then they combine in such a way that W_1 & $W_2 > W_1$ and W_1 & $W_2 > W_2$.** Proof: according to Axiom 2.2.17 (below), the strength of a want is directly proportional to the expected increment in pleasure/decrement in pain. Since, according to Axiom 2.2.25 (below), pleasures/pains combine in such a way that the combination is stronger than each of the components, it follows that wants combine in the same way as pleasures, and, hence, the corollary follows.

2.2 *Pleasure and Pain*

Definition 2.2.0 **"Pleasure" = df "The quality of awareness that persons want to attain, maintain, and increase."**

Note 2.2.1 Pleasure is used here in a completely general sense as a name for what persons want to experience. There are no other characteristics common to all pleasures. Also, there is, in principle, no limit to what could give pleasure to a person. If a saint wants to be crucified and acts according to this, it follows from Definition 2.2.0 that the saint expects more pleasure from this than, for example, from escaping the pursuers.

Definition 2.2.2 **"Pain" = df "The quality of awareness that persons want to avoid, escape from, and diminish."**

Note 2.2.3 Pain is used here in a completely general sense as a name for what persons want not to experience. There are no other characteristics common to all pains. There is, in principle, no limit to what could give pain to a person. If a saint is tempted by the Devil with all the wealth and all the possible attractions of the world and resists, preferring to be crucified, it follows from Definition 2.2.2 that the saint expects more pain from giving in to the temptation than from being crucified.

Corollary 2.2.4 **If P wants X, then P believes attainment of X will yield increment in pleasure and/or decrement in pain.** Proof: this follows directly from Definitions 2.2.0 and 2.2.2.

Corollary 2.2.5 **If P wants to avoid X, then P believes that avoidance of X will yield increment in pleasure and/or decrement in pain.** Proof: this follows directly from Definitions 2.2.0 and 2.2.2.

Corollary 2.2.6 **If P in C at t wants X instead of Y, then P believes that X will yield more pleasure and/or less pain than Y.** Proof: this follows directly from Definitions 2.2.0 and 2.2.2.

Corollary 2.2.7 **If *P* in *C* at *t* believes that *X* will yield more pleasure and/or less pain than *Y*, then *P* wants *X*.** Proof: this follows directly from Definitions 2.2.0 and 2.2.2.

Note 2.2.8 One may pose the fundamental question of *why X* gives pleasure or pain to *P*. Beyond the answer that *X* fulfills a want, which, as we have seen, applies only to a part of the cases since unwanted pleasures and pains occur, there are two types of answers at the psychological level. One is a reference to history and to a possible principle stating that things and features perceived in connection with pleasurable experiences themselves become pleasurable. This may be formalized as follows:

Theorem 2.2.9 **If *P* experiences a given degree of pleasure/pain in C_1 at t_1, then *P* will expect pleasure/pain in C_2 at t_2 to the extent that *P* is aware of similarities and differences between C_1 and C_2 which *P* takes to be relevant for expecting pleasure/pain.** Proof: according to Definition 1.2.9 the presence vs. absence of something is taken to be relevant for the project of achieving a given goal if and only if this presence vs. absence is taken to indicate a possible difference in the likelihood of achieving the goal. Hence, the likelihood involved in *P*'s expectancy of pleasure vs. pain will vary with the presence/absence of what *P* takes to be relevant similarities and differences between C_1 and C_2.

Note 2.2.10 The preceding theorem is intended to cover the case where expectancy of pleasure/pain is varied through manipulating the perceived relevant similarity between situations. It should be noted that this principle is concerned with *expected* pleasure/pain only. There remains the question of whether a situation perceived to be relevantly similar yields *actual* pleasure/pain too. The answer to this must be that judgments of relevance can be more or less correct or incorrect. Obviously, if touching metal in one situation yields electric shock, and *P* takes it for granted that since another object is also metallic, it too will yield electric shock, this may or may not be correct. However, the crucial question is whether or not something acquires the capability of evoking pleasure/pain merely through being part of an initial pleasure/pain-evoking situation. Hence, if *P* has pleasant conversations with someone in a green room, will a green room alone yield some increased pleasure? The answer to this is that if the greenness was initially taken to be relevant for the pleasure, it will yield some pleasure alone. On the other hand, if the greenness was definitely taken to be entirely circumstantial, it will not yield pleasure alone, except through evoking representations of the original conversations. Hence, there is no principle involved here, only a matter of knowing how *P* perceived the original and the new context.

Note 2.2.11 Another type of answer to the question of what leads to pleasure/pain involves the concept of *need*. A need is a disposition to develop wants and the satisfaction of a need gives rise to pleasure. "Need" differs from "want" in that it is not linked to beliefs about definite means and definite goals. A need to express him- or herself artistically may exist in a person and be merely manifested in general dissatisfaction and unrest. Given paper and crayons, the person may start to experience strong pleasure and, from then on, the person may *want* to draw. In connection with this, the general dissatisfaction and unrest may diminish. For a further comment about "need" see Note 2.2.28. Pleasure and pain may also be explained at a physiological level, but this lies outside psychology proper.

Note 2.2.12   Pleasure and pain are located on a single dimension, separated by an indifference point. Given a fixed context, a person will always prefer what is relatively more pleasurable and less painful to what is relatively less pleasurable and more painful.

Note 2.2.13   Preferences involve taking more or less inclusive contexts into account. Of particular importance is the distinction between long-term and short-term consequences of a choice. Unreflective action takes into account only the here-and-now, whereas reflective action includes a consideration of possible long-term consequences. This can be formalized as follows:

Theorem 2.2.14   **Only reflective action can take into account what the person is being told.** Proof: according to Corollary 1.3.11, reflective acting always involves reflective awareness. But, according to Axiom 1.3.15, listening to talk also always involves reflective awareness, and, hence, by implication, listening to talk is impossible without reflective awareness. Therefore, since reflective action is also impossible without reflective awareness, it follows that only the reflective actor can listen to and, hence, take into account what he or she is told.

Corollary 2.2.15   **Unreflective action cannot take into account what the person has been told.** Proof: this follows directly from Theorem 2.2.14.

Note 2.2.16   Among the implications of the preceding is that reflective action can take into account very wide contexts referred to by talk. One may include in this the person talking to him- or herself. On the other hand, unreflective action simply responds to the here-and-now situation. The prototype for this is, of course, animal behavior. One specific implication is that the reflective human actor can, sometimes, defer gratification by means of verbal representations of long-term consequences, whereas the unreflective or poorly reflective human actor may succumb to immediately present temptations.

Axiom 2.2.17   **The strength of a person's want of X is directly proportional to the amount of increment in pleasure or decrement in pain that the person believes will occur when X is attained.**

Note 2.2.18   Attempts to contradict this axiom lead to incomplete descriptions. For example, the statement *"P* wants *G* very strongly, but *P* expects only pain to result from the achievement of *G"* cannot be accepted as a complete description of a situation. One is forced to wonder why *P* wants *G* and why *P* does not want to avoid *G.*

Corollary 2.2.19   **If *P*'s want of *A* is stronger than *P*'s want of *B*, then *P* believes that the amount of increment in pleasure or decrement in pain will be higher upon attainment of *A* than upon attainment of *B.*** Proof: this follows directly from Axiom 2.2.17.

Corollary 2.2.20   **If *P* believes that the amount of increment in pleasure or decrement in pain will be higher upon attainment of *A* than upon attainment of *B*, then *P*'s want of *A* is stronger than *P*'s want of *B.*** Proof: this follows directly from Axiom 2.2.17.

Theorem 2.2.21   ***P* tries to act according to want *A* and not according to want *B* when these are in conflict, when no other wants intervene, and when the perceived likelihoods of achieving the goals of *A* and *B* are equal if, and only if, *P* believes that the amount of increment in pleasure or decrement in pain will be greater upon attaining the goal of *A* than upon attaining the goal of *B.*** Proof: (a) if *P* believes that the amount of increment in pleasure or decrement in pain will be greater upon attaining the goal of *A* than upon attaining the goal of *B,* then, according to Axiom 2.2.17, *P*'s want *A* is stronger than *P*'s want *B*; but, according to Corollary 2.1.19, if *P*'s want *A* is stronger than *P*'s want *B,* when the wants are in conflict and no other wants intervene, *P* will try to act according to *A* and not according to *B*; (b) if *P* tries to act according to *A* and not according to *B* when the wants are in conflict, no other wants interfere, and the perceived likelihoods of achieving the respective goals are equal, then, according to Corollary 2.1.20, *P*'s want *A* is stronger than *P*'s want *B.* But, if *P*'s want *A* is stronger than *P*'s want *B,* then, according to Corollary 2.2.18, *P* believes that the increment in pleasure or decrement in pain will be greater upon attaining the goal of *A* than upon attaining the goal of *B.* Hence, the equivalence stated in Theorem 2.2.21 is proved.

Note 2.2.22   It is necessary to make a distinction between attainment of the goal of a want and the fulfillment of that want. It is possible to attain a goal and be disappointed, and also to be overwhelmed. The fulfillment of a want may be defined as follows:

Definition 2.2.23   **A want is fulfilled when, and to the extent that, the expected increment in pleasure or decrement in pain occurs.**

Definition 2.2.24   **A want is frustrated when, and to the extent that, it is not fulfilled. This involves absence of expected increment in pleasure or absence of expected decrement in pain.**

Note 2.2.25 It is obviously possible for *P* to experience pleasure and pain without fulfilling or frustrating an already existing want. Examples of this are an unexpected gift or an unexpected bill.

Axiom 2.2.26 **If two pleasures/pains, P_1 and P_2, occur at the same time, they combine in such a way that $P_1 \& P_2 > P_1$, and $P_1 \& P_2 > P_2$.**

Note 2.2.27 Here, as throughout this work, the quantification of variables is very weak. More refined statements can only be arrived at through empirical work in highly specified contexts and probably will be of little general interest.

Note 2.2.28 The concept of *need* is related to, but different from the concept of want. *"P has a need for A"* may be taken to mean that if *P* were to attain *A*, then *P* would experience more pleasure or less pain than if not attaining *A*. If *P* is aware of this, the need is also a reflective or unreflective want. If, on the other hand, *P* is entirely unaware of the need, it has no direct psychological reality. It may, however, have indirect importance since it may, for example, explain a pain that *P* cannot account for. Others may become aware of it and may try to draw *P*'s attention to it or change *P*'s circumstances to fit the need better.

2.3 Beliefs

Definition 2.3.0 **"*P* in *C* at *t* believes that *X* is the case" = df "*X* is not immediately accessible to *P* in *C* at *t*, but for *P*, in *C* at *t*, *X* is the case."**

Note 2.3.1 "For *P*, *X* is the case" should not be confused with *"X exists for P,"* which is the definition of "awareness." The latter refers to an unconditional relationship. *X* is a phenomenon in *P*'s awareness, or, in the terminology adopted here, *X* is an object of awareness. If *P* is aware of *X*, it cannot be wrong that *P* is aware of *X*. A belief, on the other hand, refers to *reality* and, hence, may be correct or incorrect. Beliefs may be based on other beliefs in complex systems. The general formula is: "*P* believes that *X* is the case because *P* believes that *Y* is the case because *P* believes that . . . is the case, because *P* is or has been aware of . . . ." This means that many layers of belief are anchored, in the end, in present or past awarenesses. There is, in principle, no limit to what a person could believe.

Definition 2.3.2 **"*X* is the case" = df "*X* is consistent with everything else which is the case."**

Note 2.3.3 This does not define in other terms what is meant by "is the case," but merely introduces one necessary characteristic, namely that it must be consistent with everything else which is the case, and so on. Hence, consistency is taken as a criterion of reality in this system. What is inconsistent cannot represent a reality and cannot be acted on. If two beliefs are inconsistent, one of them or both are false. If two beliefs are consistent, they may or may not be false.

Theorem 2.3.4 **A conscious person continuously believes something.** Proof: according to Axiom 1.2.7, a conscious person is continuously acting. But, according to Definition 1.2.0, acting involves believing (taking something to be relevant), and, hence, the theorem follows.

Note 2.3.5 Just as there are reflective and unreflective wants, there are reflective and unreflective beliefs.

Definition 2.3.6 **"*P* in *C* at *t* reflectively believes that *X* is the case"** = df **"*P* in *C* at *t* believes that *X* is the case and is aware that he or she believes this."**

Theorem 2.3.7 **If *P* in *C* at *t* reflectively believes that *X* is the case, then *P* in *C* at *t* can describe and talk about that belief.** Proof: it follows from Definition 2.3.6 that if *P* in *C* at *t* reflectively believes that *X* is the case, then *P* is aware of that he or she believes that *X* is the case. But, if *P* is aware of that he or she believes that *X* is the case, then, according to Definition 1.3.0, *P* is reflectively aware of that belief. From this it follows, according to Axiom 1.3.4, that *P* in *C* at *t* can describe and talk about the belief. Hence, the theorem is proved.

Theorem 2.3.8 **If *P* in *C* at *t* can describe and talk about his or her belief that *X* is the case, then *P* reflectively believes that *X* is the case.** Proof: it follows from Axiom 1.3.4 that if *P* in *C* at *t* can describe and talk about his or her belief that *X* is the case, then *P* is reflectively aware of that belief, and, according to Definition 1.3.0, *P* is aware that he or she has the belief. But, if *P* is aware that he or she believes that *X* is the case, then, according to Definition 2.3.6, *P* reflectively believes that *X* is the case. Hence, the theorem is proved.

Note 2.3.9 Theorems 2.3.7 and 2.3.8 can be combined into an equivalence.

Note 2.3.10 *P* may very well be reflectively aware of his or her belief that *X* is the case and yet not actually describe and talk about it. Only the *ability* to describe and talk about is involved here.

Definition 2.3.11 **"*P* in *C* at *t* unreflectively believes that *X* is the case"** = df **"*P* in *C* at *t* believes that *X* is the case, but is not aware that he or she believes this."**

Theorem 2.3.12 **If *P* in *C* at *t* unreflectively believes that *X* is the case, then *P* in *C* at *t* cannot describe and talk about that belief.** Proof: it follows from Definition 2.3.11 that if *P* in *C* at *t* unreflectively believes that *X* is the case, then *P* is not aware that he or she believes this. But, if *P* believes that *X* is the case, but is not aware that he or she believes this, then, according to Definition 1.3.1, *P* is unreflectively aware of *X*. From this it follows, according to Axiom 1.3.4 that *P* in *C* at *t* cannot describe and talk about the belief that *X* is the case.

Theorem 2.3.13 **If *p* in *C* at *t* believes that *X* is the case, but cannot describe and talk about this belief, then that belief is unreflective.** Proof: it follows from Axiom 1.3.4 that if *P* in *C* at *t* cannot describe and talk about a belief, then *P* cannot be reflectively aware of this belief, but must be unreflectively aware of it. According to Definition 1.3.1, if *P* is unreflectively aware of a belief, then *P* is not aware that he or she is aware of it. But, according to Definition 2.3.11 this means that *P*'s belief is unreflective. Hence, the theorem is proved.

Note 2.3.14 Theorems 2.3.7 and 2.3.8 can be combined into an equivalence and so can Theorems 2.3.12 and 2.3.13. The conjunction of all four theorems corresponds to Axiom 1.3.4 as it applies to the domain of beliefs.

Note 2.3.15 Since it is *P* who believes, *P* cannot be unaware of a belief, in the sense of not taking it into account in actual behavior. However, *P* may be only unreflectively aware of the belief, that is, may be unable to describe it or talk about it.

Note 2.3.16 In the case of an individual with multiple personalities, P_1 may perhaps be strictly unaware of a belief or want of P_2, whereas, within one person, there must be awareness of own beliefs and wants. Unreflectively, existing beliefs and wants always guide a person's behavior. The expression "to take for granted" will be used as equivalent to "believe unreflectively."

Definition 2.3.17 **"*P*'s belief *A* is stronger than *P*'s belief *B*"** = df **"When *P*'s beliefs, *A* and *B*, are in conflict and all other factors are equal, *P* tries to act according to *A* and not according to *B*."**

Definition 2.3.18 **"Two beliefs are in conflict"** = df **"Acting according to one of the beliefs is incompatible with acting according to the other one."**

Note 2.3.19 The preference for acting in accordance with *A* and not in accordance with *B*, when the beliefs are in conflict and all other factors are equal, is a *criterion* of strength of belief. A criterion is valid by definition. It should be distinguished from a *symptom*, which is taken to be correlated with an underlying state and, hence, needs to be empirically validated.

Axiom 2.3.20 **The strength of a person's belief that *X* is the case is directly proportional to that person's estimate of the likelihood that *X* is the case.**

Note 2.3.21 Only in the case of reflective beliefs, which *P* can describe, is it possible to obtain direct estimates from *P* of the subjective likelihood that *X* is the case. The strength of unreflective beliefs may be estimated by arranging situations in which Definition 2.3.17 can be applied.

Corollary 2.3.22 **If *P*'s belief *A* is stronger than *P*'s belief *B*, then *P*'s estimate of the likelihood that *A* is correct is higher than *P*'s estimate of the likelihood that *B* is correct.** Proof: this follows directly from Axiom 2.3.20.

Corollary 2.3.23 **If *P*'s estimate of the likelihood that *A* is correct is higher than *P*'s estimate of the likelihood that *B* is correct, then *P*'s belief *A* is stronger than *P*'s belief *B*.** Proof: this follows directly from Axiom 2.3.20.

Theorem 2.3.24 ***P* tries to act according to belief *A* and not according to belief *B* when these are in conflict and all other factors are equal if, and only if, *P* believes that the likelihood of *A* being correct is higher than the likelihood of *B* being correct.** Proof: (a) if *P* tries to act according to *A* and not according to *B*, then, according to Definition 2.3.17, *P*'s belief *A* is stronger than *P*'s belief *B;* but then, according to Corollary 2.3.22, it follows that *P*'s estimate of the likelihood that *A* is correct is higher than *P*'s estimate of the likelihood that *B* is correct; (b) if *P*'s estimate of the likelihood that *A* is correct is higher than *P*'s estimate of the likelihood that *B* is correct, then, according to Axiom 2.3.20, *P*'s belief *A* is stronger than *P*'s belief *B*. But, according to Definition 2.3.17, it then follows that *P* will try to act according to *A* and not according to *B*. By this, Theorem 2.3.24 is proved.

2.4 Parallels and Interplay Between Wants and Beliefs

Note 2.4.0 There is an obvious parallel between the conceptual structures surrounding wants and beliefs. Want is to fulfillment as belief is to confirmation. Perceived goal attainment may or may not fulfill a want. Perception may or may not confirm a belief. Furthermore, perception in both cases has belief character and, hence, may be mistaken. The experience of fulfillment at having passed an exam may turn out to be premature if there was a printing error in the list of results. The belief that the exam was passed may also have been due to an erroneous perception of the list of results, which became evident by moving closer and adjusting the light.

Note 2.4.1 The analogy between wants and beliefs also extends in other directions. Pleasure is linked to the fulfillment of a want through Axiom 2.2.17. Pleasure may also be linked to the confirmation of a belief in the following way:

Axiom 2.4.2 **A person wants to believe what is the case.**

Note 2.4.3 This axiom simply asserts that there is always a want to know the truth. It asserts nothing about the strength of this want and it does not deny the possibility that other wants may occasionally be stronger. There obviously exist cases of denial and cases of reluctance to know the truth.

31

Theorem 2.4.4 **The confirmation of a belief involves an increment in pleasure.** Proof: the confirmation of a belief indicates that it corresponds to what is the case. Therefore, according to Axiom 2.4.2, confirmation is the fulfillment of a want. But, according to Definition 2.2.0, fulfillment of a want involves an increment in pleasure, and, hence, the theorem follows.

Theorem 2.4.5 **The nonconfirmation of a belief involves an increment in pain.** Proof: the nonconfirmation of a belief indicates that it does not correspond to what is the case. Therefore, according to Axiom 2.4.2, nonconfirmation is the frustration of a want. But, according to Definition 2.2.17, the frustration of a want involves pain. Hence, the theorem follows.

Corollary 2.4.6 **The fulfillment of a want involves confirmation.** Proof: according to Corollary 2.2.4 a want involves a belief that goal attainment will yield an increment in pleasure. Therefore, the pleasure accompanying goal attainment is also confirmation of a belief.

Theorem 2.4.7 *P* **wants to resolve ambiguity.** Proof: an ambiguous situation involves conflicting beliefs of undecided validity. No confirmation occurs. But, according to Theorems 2.4.4 and 2.4.5, confirmation involves increment in pleasure and nonconfirmation involves increment in pain. Therefore, the resolution of ambiguity and, hence, confirmation brings increment in pleasure and, according to Definition 2.2.0, is wanted.

Theorem 2.4.8 *P* **wants to resolve ambivalence.** Proof: an ambivalent situation involves conflicting wants of approximately equal strength. Therefore *P* cannot act, and, hence, there is no fulfillment of wants. The resolution of ambivalence means that *P* can act and, hence, achieve the fulfillment of wants and pleasure. Therefore, since, according to Definition 2.2.0, *P* wants to achieve pleasure, it follows that *P* wants to resolve ambivalence.

2.5 *Moral Wants and Beliefs*

Note 2.5.0 *Moral* wants and beliefs differ from personal wants and beliefs in that they are taken to be valid for everyone and in that there is a rigid connection between belief and want.

Axiom 2.5.1 **A person is held responsible and accountable for his or her acts by everyone involved.**

Note 2.5.2 When someone is held to be not fully responsible or quite irresponsible, that individual is, by virtue of this, partially or wholly deprived of his or her personhood. Hence, small children are generally treated as not yet fully developed persons.

Note 2.5.3 The responsibility is generally upheld both by the actor and by others. It means that the person must accept rewards and punishments for own past acts and is expected to make amends for damage caused and to accept the fruits of his or her own accomplishments. Since the record of one's past acts is so important, the future becomes very important in social life. You will be held responsible in the future for what you are doing now, which will then be the past. This responsibility discourages living in the present. *P* is also held accountable for his or her acts, which means that *P* is expected to be able to describe and explain what he or she has done in acceptable ways. *P* is held responsible for these descriptions and explanations too.

Note 2.5.4 The definition of a person as one who is able to be reflectively aware and act reflectively is intimately linked to the feature of accountability. Only because children are held increasingly accountable for their acts, do they become persons who can talk *about* what they have experienced and have done.

Axiom 2.5.5 **A person wants to do what he or she believes is morally right and wants not to do what he or she believes is morally wrong.**

Note 2.5.6 It is not asserted that a person will necessarily act morally. This also depends on the strength of the person's other beliefs and wants in the given situation at the given time. However, the axiom asserts that a moral belief always involves a moral want.

Axiom 2.5.7 **A person wants everyone to accept what he or she believes is morally right and to reject what he or she believes is morally wrong.**

Note 2.5.8 Moral beliefs are taken to be valid for everyone. This also means that it is morally right, unless higher order moral beliefs contradict it, to try to persuade others and to enforce morality. Axiom 2.5.7 does not preclude recognition of differences in moral beliefs. Example: "I think slavery is wrong, but I recognize that they regard it as right." However, the axiom assumes that if one believes slavery is wrong, then there will be a want to have it abolished.

Summary

The main determinants of awareness and action are wants and beliefs. A "want" is defined as what one would like to have, and "belief" is defined as what one takes to be the case. Both wants and beliefs may be reflective or unreflective, that is, one may or may not be aware of them. "Pleasure" is defined as the quality of awareness that a person wants, and "pain" is defined as the quality of awareness that a person does not want. "Reality" is defined in terms of consistency. What is taken to be the case is that which is consistent with other things taken to be the case, and so on. It is assumed that a person wants that which is believed to yield increment in pleasure or decrement in pain. Also, it is assumed that a person wants to believe what is the case. A fundamental characteristic of persons is that they are held accountable for their actions in terms of the moral of the culture to which they belong. It is assumed that a moral belief implies a moral want. If a person believes something is the right thing to do, then the person wants to do it. Whether or not it is actually done depends on the person's other wants and beliefs, as well as on his or her abilities. Moral beliefs are taken to be valid for everyone. Hence, unless there are other higher order rules forbidding it, it is seen as morally right to try to persuade others to behave in morally right ways.

3 Feeling

Note 3.0.0 The concept of "feeling" refers to an aspect of awareness, just as the concepts of "want" and "belief." However, the concept of "feeling" is not logically independent of the other two concepts. The criteria for correctly labeling a person's feelings are to be found in the relationship between that person's current wants and beliefs. This means that a person's feeling may be inferred from that person's wants and beliefs at the given time. Bodily and mental symptoms of feeling are also interpreted in the light of this relationship between wants and beliefs. The reader is reminded of the distinction between "criteria" and "symptoms." Criteria are logically necessary, and, taken together, sufficient indicators of the presence of a member of a category. Symptoms are empirically established probabilistic indicators, to be validated against the criteria. Wants and beliefs taken together are the criteria of feelings.

3.1 General Characteristics of Feelings

Definition 3.1.1 *"P's feeling in C at t"* = df *"P's state of awareness in C at t, as defined by the relationship between P's wants and P's beliefs."*

Note 3.1.2 To any given combination of wants and beliefs there is one, and only one, corresponding feeling state. This state may involve a "pure" feeling, describable by one term, or "mixed" feeling, describable only by more than one term. Conversely, to any given feeling there is an infinite number of corresponding possible wants and beliefs, the only constraint being that they have a given relationship to each other.

Note 3.1.3 The numerous words for feelings in natural languages come in big clusters with obviously overlapping meanings. For the purpose of systematic analysis, one needs to select a set of terms for feelings which are nonoverlapping in meaning or, in other words, conceptually independent. The test for conceptual independence goes as follows: assuming that *P* in *C* at *t* has or does not have feeling *A(B)*, does it necessarily follow from this that *P* in *C* at *t* also has or does not have feeling **B(A)**? If nothing definite follows either way, then the conclusion is that *A* and *B* are conceptually independent of each other. Examples: suppose that *P* is happy or unhappy. Does it necessarily follow from either of these that *P* is delighted or not delighted? And, conversely, does it necessarily follow from *P* being delighted or not delighted that *P* is happy or unhappy? The answer is clearly that one cannot be happy without being at all delighted and one cannot be delighted without being at all happy. Similarly, it does not make sense to say that someone is completely unhappy and delighted, or not at all delighted, yet happy. The conclusion is that these terms are not conceptually independent.

Consider now the pair of terms "angry" and "ashamed": if someone is angry or not angry, it does not necessarily follow that he or she is also ashamed or not ashamed. Similarly, if someone is ashamed or not ashamed, it does not necessarily follow that he or she is angry or not angry. Hence, these two terms are conceptually independent. The impressionistic method used here to assess conceptual independence may be improved upon in two ways. One is to study the extent to which informants actually treat the concepts as independent, given concrete examples. The other is to provide strict definitions of the concepts and investigate their formal logical relationship.

Note 3.1.4 Mixing of feelings should not be confused with conceptual dependence. A person may very well be half ashamed and half angry, although these feelings are conceptually independent. Actually, it only makes sense to talk about mixed feelings, when the ingredients *are* conceptually independent. It makes little sense to say that a person feels partly happy and partly delighted. The terminology of mixing of feelings implies a constraint on total capacity for feeling. One can be half angry and half ashamed, but one cannot be maximally angry and maximally ashamed at the same time. This means that increasing one feeling may be a way of decreasing another – making someone very angry makes that person less anxious, and so on. This may be formalized as follows:

Axiom 3.1.5 **The sum of the strengths of a person's feelings at a given moment has an upper limit equal to the maximum possible strength of any single feeling at that moment.**

Note 3.1.6 Since our measures of the strength of feelings are usually very crude, only a few general implications may be drawn from Axiom 3.1.5. Two of the most frequently used of these are as follows:

Corollary 3.1.7 **If the strength of one of a person's feelings at a given moment is maximal, then that person can have only that one feeling at that moment.**
Proof: this follows directly from Axiom 3.1.5.

Corollary 3.1.8 **If the sum of the strengths of a person's feelings at a given moment is close to maximal, then an increase in the strength of one of the feelings will be accompanied by a decrease in the strength of one or several of the others.** Proof: this follows directly from Axiom 3.1.5.

3.2 Reflectivity of Feelings

Note 3.2.1 Feelings may be unreflective or reflective. In the former case, they may only be inferred, with certainty, from knowledge of the relationship between the person's wants and beliefs and, probabilistically, from various symptoms. In the latter case they may also be described and talked about by the person who harbors them.

Definition 3.2.2 **"*P* in *C* at *t* has a reflective feeling"** = df **"*P* in *C* at *t* has a feeling and is aware that he or she has it."**

Definition 3.2.3 **"*P* in *C* at *t* has an unreflective feeling"** = df **"*P* in *C* at *t* has a feeling and is not aware that he or she has it."**

Corollary 3.2.4 **If *P* in *C* at *t* has a reflective feeling, then *P* in *C* at *t* can describe and talk about that feeling.** Proof: this follows directly from Axiom 1.3.4.

Corollary 3.2.5 **If *P* in *C* at *t* can describe and talk about a feeling, then *P* in *C* at *t* has a reflective feeling.** Proof: this follows directly from Axiom 1.3.4.

Corollary 3.2.6 **If *P* in *C* at *t* has an unreflective feeling, then *P* in *C* at *t* cannot describe and talk about that feeling.** Proof: this follows directly from Axiom 1.3.4.

Corollary 3.2.7 **If *P* in *C* at *t* cannot describe and talk about a feeling, then *P* in *C* at *t* has an unreflective feeling.** Proof: this follows directly from Axiom 1.3.4.

Note 3.2.8 Corollaries 3.2.4, 3.2.5, 3.2.6, and 3.2.7 together are equivalent to Axiom 1.3.4 as it applies to feelings.

Note 3.2.9 Since feelings are defined by the relationship between wants and beliefs, it follows that a person may have an inappropriate feeling, corresponding to an inappropriate want and/or an inappropriate belief.

Note 3.2.10 Since *P* is the one who feels, it makes no sense to state that *P* is unaware of his or her feelings. However, *P* may not be aware *that* he or she has these feelings, and, hence, the awareness may only be unreflective. Again, the distinction between criteria and symptoms is important. An unreflective feeling may be expressed in various bodily and behavioral symptoms, but the interpretation of these symptoms must rely on the criteria of the various feelings. Only if a given relationship between wants and beliefs is known to be present can a given set of bodily and behavioral symptoms be interpreted as reflecting a particular feeling.

Note 3.2.11 Comparing the analyses given so far with those on wants and beliefs above, it should be evident that feelings do not yield any additional information compared to what is gained from studying wants and beliefs. This follows from the definition of "feelings" as consisting of the relationship between wants and beliefs. Feelings are simply a very convenient way of ordering the want-belief relations into certain classes.

Note 3.2.12 Since feelings consist of a relationship between wants and beliefs, the Distinction between reflective and unreflective becomes somewhat more complicated with them. Feelings involving only reflective wants and reflective beliefs may be called "reflective feelings" (see Definition 3.2.2). Similarly, feelings involving only unreflective wants and beliefs may be called "unreflective feelings" (Definition 3.2.3). Feelings in which either the want or the belief, but not both, are reflective, may be called "partly reflective feelings." The following definition applies:

Definition 3.2.13 **"P in C at t has a partly reflective feeling"** = df **"P in C at t has a feeling involving a reflective want or a reflective belief, but not both."**

Note 3.2.14 The distinctions involved in Definitions 3.2.2, 3.2.3, and 3.2.13 are simplified since they do not involve continuous degrees of reflectivity. Nevertheless, they suffice to characterize some common cases. Most feelings are such that the person is, or can be, clearly aware of the wants and likelihoods involved. Example: I am afraid because the likelihood that I will soon sit in the dentist's chair is very high and I want very much to avoid the pain involved. This is a reflective feeling as described in Definition 3.2.2. An example of a partly reflective feeling is the following: I feel sad when I think of that wonderful woman. I know that I want her very much. But, why does that make me sad? Obviously, because I regard her as completely unattainable. I had not thought of that. Another example: I feel sad when I think about that wonderful man. I know that he is completely unattainable. But why should that make me sad? Obviously, because I really want to have him. I had not thought of that. Unreflective feelings may often be discovered by others, through inference from the person's wants, beliefs, or behavior. To the extent that unreflective wants and beliefs exist, so must unreflective feelings.

3.3 Strength of Feelings

Definition 3.3.1 **"The strength of a feeling F"** = df **"The product of the strength of the want and the strength of the belief whose relationship constitutes the feeling F."**

Note 3.3.2 The strength of feelings, wants, and beliefs can usually only be measured in ordinal scales. They tend to change constantly and are hard to compare across contexts and over time. Consequently, only certain very crude predictions may be derived from Definition 3.3.1. W, want; B, belief; and F, feeling.

Corollary 3.3.3 **If $W_1 > W_2$ and $B_1 =$ or $> B_2$, then $F_1 (= W_1 \times B_1) > F_2 (= W_2 \times B_2)$.** Proof: this follows directly from Definition 3.3.1.

Corollary 3.3.4 **If $W_1 =$ or $> W_2$ and $B_1 > B_2$, then $F_1 (= W_1 \times B_1) > F_2 (= W_2 \times B_2)$.** Proof: this follows directly from Definition 3.3.1.

Note 3.3.5 These corollaries contain two parallel assertions. One is that if a want, W_1, is stronger than another want, W_2, and the belief B_1, concerning the likelihood of attaining the goal of W_1, is not weaker than the belief B_2, concerning the likelihood of attaining the goal of W_2, then the feeling F_1 corresponding to W_1 and B_1 is stronger than the feeling F_2 corresponding to W_2 and B_2. For example, the happiness upon being informed that one has won \$ 20000 is stronger than the happiness upon being informed that one has won \$ 1000, at least when the trustworthiness of the former information is taken to be stronger than, or equally as high as, the trustworthiness of the latter information. It can easily be seen that the relative strength of happiness becomes less predictable when the information that one has won \$ 20000 is seen as highly doubtful, whereas the information about having won \$ 1000 is taken to be virtually certain. The other assertion of the corollaries is that if a belief, B_1, in the likelihood of attaining the goal of W_1 is stronger than the belief B_2 in the likelihood of attaining the goal of W_2, and W_1 is not weaker than W_2, then the feeling F_1, corresponding to W_1 and B_1, is stronger than the feeling F_2, corresponding to W_2 and B_2. For example, the happiness upon being informed that one has almost certainly won a sum of money is greater than the happiness upon being informed that there is a remote possibility that one has won a sum of money, at least when the sum allegedly won in the former case is not smaller than the sum allegedly won in the latter case.

Note 3.3.6 Another way of expressing the preceding is to say that the strength of a feeling is directly and monotonically related to the strength of the corresponding want, when the corresponding belief is held constant, and to the corresponding belief when the corresponding want is held constant.

Definition 3.3.7 **"P's feeling A is stronger than P's feeling B in C at t"** = df **"If, when P's feelings A and B are in conflict in C at t, P acts according to the wants and beliefs constituting A rather than according to the wants and beliefs constituting B."**

Definition 3.3.8 **"P's feelings A and B are in conflict"** = df **"The wants and the beliefs**

39

constituting *P*'s feeling *A* and the wants and beliefs constituting *P*'s feeling *B* lead to incompatible acts."

Note 3.3.9   In a situation in which fear would lead *P* to run, whereas pride would lead *P* to stay (and avoid shame), then running or staying indicates which feeling is strongest.

Corollary 3.3.10   **If *P* in *C* at *t* has a reflective feeling *F* and if *P* judges his or her own ratings of the strength of *F* to be adequate, then *P*'s ratings of the strength of *F* will be directly and monotonically related to the actual strength of *F*.** Proof: it follows from Corollary 1.3.23 that *P*'s ratings will be correct. But if they are correct, they must be directly and monotonically related to what is rated.

Note 3.3.11   The above is an example of the validity by definition of reports of subjective experience when the reports are experienced by the person as adequate.

Note 3.3.12   Definitions 3.3.1 and 3.3.7 and Corollary 3.3.10 indicate three different ways of gauging the strength of a feeling. These are, through the product of the strengths of the wants and beliefs linked with the feeling, through its dominance over other feelings, and through direct ratings by the person involved. The last method is only available in the case of reflective feelings. The joint implications of these methods may be formulated in the following three theorems:

Theorem 3.3.13   **If *P*'s feelings F_1 and F_2 in *C* at *t* are in conflict and *P* acts according to F_1, then the product of the strengths of the wants and beliefs constituting F_1 is greater than the product of the strengths of the wants and beliefs constituting F_2.** Proof: according to Definition 3.3.7, if two feelings are in conflict and *P* acts according to the wants and beliefs constituting one of them and not according to the wants and beliefs constituting the other, then the first feeling is stronger than the second. But, according to Definition 3.3.1, the strength of a feeling is equal to the product of the strengths of the wants and beliefs constituting the feeling. Hence, Theorem 3.3.13 follows.

Theorem 3.3.14   **If *P*'s reflective feelings F_1 and F_2 in *C* at *t* are in conflict and *P* acts according to F_1, then *P* in *C* at *t* will rate F_1 as being stronger than F_2.** Proof: according to Definition 3.3.7, if two feelings are in conflict and *P* acts according to one of them, then that feeling is stronger than the other one. But, according to Corollary 3.3.10, if one reflective feeling is stronger than another, *P* will rate that feeling as stronger than the other. Hence, Theorem 3.3.14 follows.

Theorem 3.3.15   **If the product of the strengths of the want and the belief constituting *P*'s reflective feeling F_1 in *C* at *t* is greater than the product of the strengths of the want and the belief constituting *P*'s reflective feeling F_2 in *C* at *t*,** then P in C at t will rate F_1 as stronger than F_2. Proof: according to Definition 3.3.1, the strength of a feeling equals the product of the strengths of the want and the belief constituting that feeling. Hence, F_1 is stronger than F_2. But, according to Corollary 3.3.10, if one reflective feeling is stronger than another P will rate that feeling as stronger than the other. Hence, Theorem 3.3.15 follows.

Note 3.3.16   A major distinction is between positive and negative feelings. The former involve pleasure and the latter involve pain. However, the concepts of positive and negative feeling do not coincide with the concepts of pleasure and pain. The relationship is one of inclusion, that is, positive and negative feelings are subclasses of pleasure and pain. If P has a positive feeling, then P experiences pleasure, but P may experience some pleasure without having a positive feeling. For example, P may taste a good dessert or see a beautiful landscape while being deeply unhappy. Similarly, if P has a negative feeling, then P experiences pain, but P may experience some pain without having a negative feeling. For example, P may suffer some pain at the dentist's office while being jubilantly happy. Feelings are states involving the *whole* person, whereas some pleasures and pains are limited piecemeal experiences. Obviously, the distinction between a piecemeal pleasure or pain and a feeling involving the whole person is gradual. If a landscape is very beautiful, one's unhappiness may recede for a while, and if the pain at the dentist's office is very strong, one's happiness may recede for a while. The preceding deviates from some traditional hedonistic terminology.

3.4 Positive Feelings

Note 3.4.1   It is difficult to subdivide the positive feelings in such a way that each of the resulting feelings is conceptually independent of all of the others. At least for the time being, this effort has been abandoned, and only one positive feeling will be included, namely *happiness*.

Definition 3.4.2   *"P is happy in C at t"*= df *"P believes that at least one of P's wants in C at t is being or is going to be fulfilled."*

Definition 3.4.3   *"P's degree of happiness in C at t is directly proportional to the product of the strength of the want involved and the subjective likelihood of actual fulfillment of the want."*

Note 3.4.4   Definition 3.4.2 equals happiness to the belief in the fulfillment of a want. This makes it meaningful to talk about illusory or mistaken happiness since the belief may be wrong. Definition 3.4.3 asserts that the degree of happiness is directly proportional to the product of the strength of the want and the belief. However, this is only an ideal model. Rarely, if ever, can we measure wants and beliefs on ratio or even interval scales. As has been pointed out earlier, products of ordinally measured variables involve some consequences, mostly in the form of predictions about the outcome of certain paired comparisons; cf. Corollaries 3.3.3 and 3.3.4 dealing with the relative strength of a feeling as a function of the relative strengths of the beliefs and wants involved. These also apply to the degree of happiness.

Note 3.4.5 It is common knowledge that happiness is transitory under many conditions. This has to do with the link to fulfillment of a want. A want is fulfilled within a limited time span and, as it is fulfilled, it also diminishes in strength and disappears. This may be expressed in the following theorem:

Theorem 3.4.6 **When no other wants and beliefs intervene, the amount of happiness reaches a maximum at the onset of a believed certainty of fulfillment of a want and then diminishes toward zero.** Proof: according to Definition 3.3.1, P's degree of happiness is directly proportional to the product of the strength of P's want and the subjective likelihood of actual fulfillment of the want. It follows from this that the degree of happiness reaches a maximum at the moment when the strength of the want has not yet started to diminish, but when the subjective likelihood has turned into certainty. This is the moment when the product of the strengths of the belief and the want reaches a maximum. After this, the fulfillment leads to a weakening of the want and, hence, to a weakening of the product of the strengths of want and belief and, therefore, of happiness. By this, Theorem 3.4.6 is proved.

Note 3.4.7 Cases of apparently lasting happiness may seem to pose a problem for the present position. However, several types of interpretation are possible. Some recurrent postachievement happiness may be mediated by recalling the achievement of the goal and the pleasure and happiness associated with it. Alleged cases of stable happiness often involve global characterizations of a person's life over a period of time. When closely inspected, this may involve continuously occurring and often recurrent fulfillments of many wants, each of which instigates some transitory happiness as postulated by Theorem 3.4.6.

Note 3.4.8 The transitory character of happiness is a fundamental aspect of human life and poses a constant strategic problem. "How shall I organize my life in order to create as much happiness as possible"? Not only is the fulfillment of a want followed by diminishing happiness, but repeated fulfillments of the same want under the same circumstances often seem to weaken the want and, hence, the happiness generated. Some further explications of implicitly known circumstances may be possible here.

3.5 Negative Feelings

Note 3.5.1 It is possible to discern among the numerous terms designating negative feelings a system of at least nine feelings which are conceptually independent of each other. These are *boredom, anger, fear, shame, guilt, sadness, envy, suspiciousness, disgust.* This list may be shortened or lengthened according to one's degree of emphasis on strict conceptual independence and depending on how one defines these terms. Different natural languages may yield partly different lists. However, all the feelings suggested here are defined by a particular relationship between the person's wants and beliefs.

Definition 3.5.2 **"*P* in *C* at *t* is bored"** = df **"*P* believes that he or she cannot fulfill or act toward a future fulfillment of any want in *C* at *t*, *C* at *t* is not, for *P*, the occasion for any other want, and *P* does not expect to be able to leave *C* for some time."**

Note 3.5.3 A boring situation is one in which there is nothing to do, yet one cannot leave immediately. The reason why there is nothing to do is that there is nothing one wants or believes is relevant for something one wants. The boring situation is not an occasion for any other feelings. It should be emphasized that the boring situation is seen as temporary, that is, no options are seen as permanently excluded. If the situation had been seen as permanent, there would have been sadness; see below. It follows from the definition of "boredom," as from the definitions of all negative feelings, that one wants to escape from them.

Note 3.5.4 People are susceptible to boredom to very different degrees. It must be assumed that these differences reflect their wants and beliefs and their ability to extract or create interesting tasks out of seemingly barren situations. Folk psychology has rich intuitions in this area, especially in connection with waiting rooms. Usually such rooms are provided with pictures on the walls, a rich supply of magazines, and maybe background music. When these props are insufficient, people try to engage in planning, daydreaming, or conversation.

Definition 3.5.5 **"*P* in *C* at *t* is angry"** = df **"*P* in *C* at *t* believes that he or she has intentionally or through inexcusable neglect been treated without consideration (without respect), and he or she wants to undo this (retaliate)."**

Note 3.5.6 To be treated with respect will be discussed further in Chapter 5. It means being accorded the basic rights and duties one is entitled to. This may include being treated justly, politely, considerately, and also being expected to be just, polite, and considerate oneself. Believed lack of respect is the occasion for anger, which also includes a want to *retaliate*. This essentially means to try to *force* the other one to apologize and to become respectful again ("get even"). "Indignation" is a word for anger when it is particularly felt to be morally well justified.

Note 3.5.7 People differ in the amount and kind of respect they feel entitled to, and in the amount and kind of respect they think particular others are entitled to. The differences may be quite idiosyncratic or they may be linked with differences in opinion about how factors such as age, title, wealth, caste, accomplishments, and so on determine what is appropriately respectful behavior. More than any other feeling, anger is prone to arise from misunderstanding. This follows from the assumption that people, normally, want to treat each other respectfully. Therefore, since intentional disrespect can be expected to be relatively rare while anger is quite common the latter must frequently be based on misunderstanding.

Corollary 3.5.8 **The strength of P's anger in C at t is directly proportional to the amount of intentional or indefensibly thoughtless disrespect P believes he or she has encountered in C at t.** Proof: this follows from Definition 3.5.5.

Note 3.5.9 Anger should not be confused with aggression which is acting intended to inflict pain and harm. Although anger is often expressed through aggressive acts, there is no necessary link between them. You may act aggressively without being angry, either in order to fake anger, or for other reasons. For example, a soldier may act under orders to kill and destroy while feeling only disgust at what he is doing. You may also be angry without displaying aggression because it is not regarded as prudent to do so. For example, acting aggressively may be regarded as too dangerous, or in some other way unwise.

Theorem 3.5.10 **If P in C at t is angry, then P in C at t is frustrated.** Proof: according to Definition 3.5.5, if P is angry, then P believes he or she has been treated with disrespect. But, according to Theorem 5.2.3, persons want to be treated with respect. Therefore, P's want to be treated with respect is not fulfilled, and, hence, P is frustrated. By this, Theorem 3.5.10 is proved.

Note 3.5.11 Theorem 3.5.10 is the only valid core of the original frustration-aggression hypothesis. That hypothesis was formulated with a disregard for what was common knowledge.

Definition 3.5.12 **"P in C at t is afraid"** = df **"P in C at t believes that, regardless of what he or she does, there is a definite probability that he or she will be hurt (will experience pain)."**

Note 3.5.13 The definition states that there is a believed danger and that one's personal powers are believed to be insufficient to avert it. From this it follows that the weaker a person sees him- or herself, the more frequently will that person be afraid. It also follows that persons who tend to see the world as full of dangers will be more often afraid than those who see few dangers.

Note 3.5.14 Persons may conquer their fear in two types of contexts. One is when their want to reach a particular goal is stronger than their want to avoid the possible pain. This may be exemplified by the behavior of the gold seekers who went to California in spite of the numerous dangers involved. The other context is when the want to be courageous (and the fear of shame) is stronger than the want to avoid the possible danger. This is the content of heroic tales, whether fictional or based on reality.

Note 3.5.15 Fear should not be confused with fearful behavior. Fear can be faked and fear can be hidden, according to what the person wants most strongly. There are very noticeable variations in *when* people become afraid and in *how* afraid they become. This may reflect what wants people have, and/or how they interpret the situation.

Definition 3.5.16 **"*P* in *C* at *t* feels ashamed" = df "*P* in *C* at *t* believes that he or she has been observed doing something which ought not to be done in public, either because it is not regarded as seemly or because it is done incompetently."**

Note 3.5.17 People can also feel ashamed of themselves privately if they have done something which they would be ashamed to have others know. Shame is the feeling one has when one's performance and appearance deviates from acceptable standards. The ashamed person believes that others see him or her as ridiculous and fears being ridiculed. A person who is particularly afraid of ridicule may become unusually *shy* or unusually *aggressive*. By being shy one has a chance of avoiding attention and, hence, ridicule, and by being aggressive one has a chance of scaring others from treating one disrespectfully.

Note 3.5.18 A person's shame is stronger the more important the observers are in his or her life, that is, the more their opinions make a difference to him or her. The display of unseemly or incompetent behavior to complete strangers, that is, to people who do not know you and whom you will not see again, creates comparatively little shame. Conversely, when you are very ashamed of something you have done and this is known to everyone in your surroundings, it may be a very heavy burden to live with. Shame is a feeling centering on oneself as one believes others see one.

Definition 3.5.19 **"*P* in *C* at *t* feels guilt" = df "*P* believes that he or she has done something wrong to someone."**

Note 3.5.20 Guilt always has to do with wrongdoing against one or more *persons*. It may be one particular person, a group of persons, people in a country, people in general, oneself, God, or a pet or other animal. In the latter cases, God and the animals are seen as having person-like characteristics, such as being aware, being capable of suffering, being able to feel rejected and maltreated, being capable of love, and so on.

Note 3.5.21 Persons differ greatly in the prominence of guilt feelings in their lives. This must be related, on the one hand, to their tendency to actually transgress their own norms, and on the other hand, to their tendency to attribute responsibility to themselves, rather than to other people, or to impersonal circumstances.

Note 3.5.22 Guilt feelings are characterized by the difficulty of alleviating them since they concern something past. Only a few alternatives are open for the sufferer of guilt. In a few cases, it may be possible to, literally, undo the deed, and even obliterate all traces of it. In other cases, you may offer compensations and consolations of various sorts to the victim. You may also undergo self-imposed or legally imposed penalties which may be seen as having a cleansing effect. You have suffered your punishment and now you have a clean conscience again. Finally, you may ask to be forgiven. Genuine forgiving may be felt like a blessing, but there are always doubts, and the board is never wiped entirely clean. Some record is usually kept and newborn saints are still have-been sinners.

Definition 3.5.23 **"*P* in *C* at *t* feels sad" = df "*P* in *C* at *t* believes that something he or she wants to attain has become, and will remain, forever unattainable, or something he or she has wanted to keep has been irrevocably lost."**

Note 3.5.24 Sadness involves a lack of hope, a belief that something one wants will forever remain unattainable. It also involves a *passivity,* reflecting the belief that nothing can be done. Crying is a universal expression of sadness (grief, sorrow).

Note 3.5.25 There is a particular variant of sadness which has to do with a person's total life situation and which is usually labeled *"depression."* A person may be sad because of something that has happened, but this feeling will normally diminish after a while. However, if the sadness has to do with a stable and apparently unchangeable life situation or with faults in one's own personality, it is likely to persevere for longer periods of time. Depression may be defined as follows:

Definition 3.5.26 **"*P* in *C* at *t* feels depressed" = df "*P* in *C* at *t* believes that his or her lot in life can never be improved in the way he or she wants it to be, or he or she can never become the sort of person he or she wants to be."**

Note 3.5.27 It can be seen from Definitions 3.5.23 and 3.5.26 that depression is a subclass of sadness. Hence, if a person is depressed, then he or she is sad, but a person may be sad without being depressed.

Note 3.5.28 Depression may develop in persons living under conditions of endemic poverty, hunger, and unemployment. Here, it is attributed to conditions beyond the power of individuals to change. Depression is also frequent in periods of human life when great changes are taking place. In young people there may be depression because they believe that they are unable to become the persons they would like to be. They believe they do not have and never will have the looks, the charm, the abilities, the opportunities that they would like to have. In old age, there may be depression because of seemingly irreversible loss of health, physical and mental agility, attractiveness, possibilities, and so on.

Definition 3.5.29   **"*P* in *C* at *t* is envious of *Q*"** = df **"*P* in *C* at *t* wants to have what *Q* has and wants *Q* not to have it."**

Note 3.5.30   Envy is not regarded as a nice feeling since it may accompany immoral acts of taking things away from other persons. It depends on a belief that the other person has things you yourself want and do not have. Frequently, the envy may be morally justified by the argument that the other one does not deserve what he or she has whereas you deserve to have it.

Definition 3.5.31   **"*P* in *C* at *t* is suspicious"** = df **"*P* in *C* at *t* believes that something may not be what it seems to be and wants to know what it is."**

Note 3.5.32   Although the term "suspicious" is used in every content area, in accordance with Definition 3.5.31 its main application is in the area of interpersonal relations. Suspicion is the feeling aroused when the possibility is entertained that another person is deceiving you, lying, faking, simulating, and so on. Highly suspicious persons find many occasions for doubting the sincerity of what is socially expressed.

Note 3.5.33   The definition of "suspiciousness" includes a want to know. This is derived from Axiom 2.4.2 which expresses a fundamental characteristic of persons, namely that they want to believe what is the case; cf. also the phenomenon of intolerance of ambiguity (Corollary 2.4.7). If a person lives in a continuing state of uncertainty with regard to what is going on, suspiciousness will be a prominent and recurrent feeling for that person.

Definition 3.5.34   **"*P* in *C* at *t* feels disgusted with *X*"** = df **"*P* in *C* at *t* is in contact with *X*, and this is incompatible with *P*'s moral and/or esthetic and/or hygienic standards."**

Note 3.5.35   The feeling of disgust (revulsion) is clearly related to some notion of cleanliness or pollution. It has to do with being a decent person and responding aversely to what is indecent and outside the boundaries of what is acceptable. There are socially imposed standards of personal hygiene, eating and drinking habits, sexual behavior, religious behavior, and so on. The more blatant the deviations from these standards, the stronger one's disgust. Although the linguistic metaphors clearly have to do with the body, the feeling of disgust can be as prominent in reactions to, for example, political or religious messages.

Note 3.5.36 Interpersonally, disgust is associated with wholesale rejection of a person. It may well be that the message of tolerance in modern society masks a lot of unreflective disgust. Complete tolerance would turn people into caricatures and society into chaos. Socialized individuals always have standards and deviation from these always creates disgust.

Note 3.5.37 Feeling terms summarize and evaluate the relationship between the person and the situation from the person's point of view. It is a matter of logical necessity that the relationship between feelings and action is much closer than that between wants and action or between beliefs and action. This follows because feelings as well as action are the outcomes of *both* wants *and* beliefs. The next chapter will present the logic of action.

Summary

"Feeling" is defined as a state of awareness determined by the momentary relationship between a person's wants and a person's beliefs. The person may not be aware that he or she has a feeling. A person may at any moment have only one feeling or a mixture of feelings. Feelings are not regarded as separate entities with particular bodily and/or behavioral symptoms, but are simply a convenient way of ordering want-belief relations into classes. Feelings may be positive or negative. Positive feelings involve pleasure, but one may experience pleasure without having a positive feeling. Similarly, negative feelings involve pain, but one may experience pain without having a negative feeling. Feelings are states of the whole person, whereas pleasure and pain may also be localized experiences, such as a good taste or a toothache. A major positive feeling is happiness. It occurs when a person believes that a want is or is going to be satisfied. Happiness is transient and has to be continuously sought for. Negative feelings occur when a person believes that a want is or is going to be frustrated. Nine negative feelings, all conceptually independent of each other, are defined and described. These are boredom, anger, fear, shame, guilt, sadness, envy, suspiciousness, and disgust.

4 Acting

Note 4.0.0 In this chapter the conditions for acting will be treated. For a definition and discussion of the concept of acting itself, the reader is referred to Chapter 1.

Note 4.0.1 In what follows the central terms *"can"* and *"try"* are left formally undefined. Nevertheless, it should be clear from everyday usage that *"P can do A"* means "it is possible for P to do A," and that *"P tries to do A"* means *"P attempts to do A"* (*"P makes an effort to do A"*).

4.1 The General Conditions of Acting

Axiom 4.1.0 **A person P does A in the context C at time t if, and only if, P can do A in C at t and P tries to do A in C at t.**

Corollary 4.1.1 **If P does not do A in C at t, then P cannot do A in C at t, or P does not try to do A in C at t, or P neither can nor tries to do A in C at t.** Proof: this follows directly from Axiom 4.1.0.

Corollary 4.1.2 **If P can do A in C at t and P does not do A in C at t, then P does not try to do A in C at t.** Proof: this follows directly from Axiom 4.1.0.

Corollary 4.1.3 **If P tries to do A in C at t and P does not do A in C at t, then P cannot do A in C at t.** Proof: this follows directly from Axiom 4.1.0.

Note 4.1.4 Axiom 4.1.0 and its corollaries are very frequently used in everyday life. The conclusions about "can" and "try" also frequently form the basis for more or less uncertain generalizations about the person's abilities, beliefs, and wants.

4.2 The Conditions of Can

Axiom 4.2.0 **A person P can do A in the context C at time t if, and only if, P's ability to do A in C at t exceeds the difficulty of doing A in C at t.**

Note 4.2.1 Ability is a person-variable, and difficulty is a task-variable. If the task is to jump over an obstacle, *P*'s ability to jump is a person-variable, and the height of the obstacle is a task-variable. It should be clear that these factors can be varied independently of each other. In what follows *P* and *Q* are persons and *T* and *R* are tasks.

Definition 4.2.2 **P in C at t has greater ability relative to task T than Q in C at t, if, in C at t, P succeeds and Q fails on T; or P succeeds on T with less exertion than Q; or, when both P and Q succeed on T, it takes less increment in the difficulty of T to make Q fail than it takes to make P fail; or, when both P and Q fail, it takes less decrement in the difficulty of T to make P succeed than it takes to make Q succeed.**

Note 4.2.3 The preceding definition contains four *criteria* of relative strength of an ability. Here "ability" is defined relative to one task only. Conventional concepts of ability are generalized over categories of tasks and rely on probability of success rather than on simple pass and fail. Even so, these conventional concepts are not inconsistent with the elementary criteria presented here, but, on the contrary, presuppose them.

Definition 4.2.4 **T is more difficult than R for P in C at t if, in C at t, P fails on T and succeeds on R; or P succeeds on T with more exertion than on R; or, when P succeeds on both tasks, it takes less decrement in P's ability to make him or her fail on T than it takes to make him or her fail on R; or, when P fails on both tasks, it takes more increment in P's ability to make him or her succeed on T than it takes to make him or her succeed on R.**

Note 4.2.5 The preceding definition contains four *criteria* of the relative difficulty of tasks for a person. Conventional measures of difficulty are generalized over many persons and measure difficulty in terms of probability of passing. However, these conventional measures do not contradict the fundamental concept of difficulty presented in Definition 4.2.4, but, on the contrary, presuppose it.

Note 4.2.6 It does *not* follow from Definitions 4.2.2 and 4.2.4 that the relative difficulties of tasks are ordered in the same way for different persons, or that the relative abilities of persons are ordered in the same way for different tasks. Nor does it follow that the order found at a given time will be maintained at a later time. Definitions 4.2.2 and 4.2.4 also do not deny such ordering. The study of ability and difficulty is clearly a matter for empirical research.

Axiom 4.2.7 **The degree of exertion of a person P in performing A in the context C at time t is inversely proportional to the size of the positive difference between the ability of P to perform A in C at t and the difficulty for P of A in C at t.**

Note 4.2.8 A positive difference exists as long as the ability is higher than the difficulty. When there is a negative difference, that is, when the ability is lower than the difficulty, *P* can no longer perform *A*. As the positive difference becomes greater, the amount of necessary exertion declines. Axiom 4.2.7 formulates a *criterion* of exertion.

Note 4.2.9 *Symptoms* of exertion include physical tension, facial and bodily expressions of effort, preoccupation, lowered tolerance of disturbance, slowed performance, heightened frequency of errors and corrections, and the person's own statement about how it feels or felt to perform *A*. The latter symptom applies only when the act is reflective. The following corollaries may be formulated concerning the relation between difficulty, ability, and exertion:

Corollary 4.2.10 **If *P* must exert him- or herself very much to perform *A* in *C* at *t*, then *P*'s ability to perform *A* in *C* at *t* is only a little higher than the difficulty for *P* of *A* in *C* at *t*.** Proof: this follows directly from Axiom 4.2.7.

Corollary 4.2.11 **If *P* must exert him- or herself very little to perform *A* in *C* at *t*, then *P*'s ability to perform *A* in *C* at *t* is much higher than the difficulty for *P* of *A* in *C* at *t*.** Proof: this follows directly from Axiom 4.2.7.

Corollary 4.2.12 **If *P* performs *A* in *C* at *t* with little exertion and *Q* performs *A* in *C* at *t* with great exertion, then, if no other circumstances intervene, *P* must have higher ability than *Q* in performing *A* in *C* at *t*.** Proof: this follows directly from Axiom 4.2.7.

Corollary 4.2.13 **If *P* manages to perform *A* in *C* at *t* only with great exertion and if *P* has much higher ability than *Q* for doing *A* in *C* at *t*, then it is very likely that *A* in *C* at *t* is too difficult for *Q*.** Proof: this follows directly from Axiom 4.2.7.

Corollary 4.2.14 **If *P* performs *A* in *C* at *t* with little exertion and if *P* has lower ability than *Q*, then *A* in *C* at *t* must be very easy for *Q*.** Proof: this follows directly from Axiom 4.2.7.

Note 4.2.15 The preceding summarizes some of the conditions of can. It should be noted that the formulas contain no generalizations. The permissible inferences are limited to the same persons, contexts, time periods, and acts. These formulations are very useful and much used in everyday life. The next theme is the conditions of trying.

4.3 The Conditions of Trying

Axiom 4.3.1 **A person *P* tries to do *A* in the context *C* at time *t* if, and only if, *A* is the act which, for *P* in *C* at *t*, has the highest expected utility.**

Definition 4.3.2 **"*A* has the highest expected utility for *P* in *C* at *t*"**= df **"*A* is the act**

which for P in C at t has the highest product of the expected outcome pleasure and the likelihood of leading to that outcome."

Note 4.3.3 The concept of "pleasure" used in the preceding definition corresponds very well to the concept of "value" which is usually part of the expected utility function; cf. Definition 2.2.0 which states that pleasure is the quality of awareness that persons want to attain, maintain, and increase.

Note 4.3.4 Even in the simplest choice situation of doing A vs. not doing A, there are at least ten variables involved, all logically independent of each other. First, there is the subjective likelihood that A leads to G. This also logically determines the likelihood that A leads to *not-G*. Next, there is the subjective likelihood that *not-A* leads to G. This also logically determines the likelihood that *not-A* leads to *not-G*. Furthermore, there is the subjective value of G given A, the subjective value of G, given *not-A*, the subjective value of *not-G* given A, and the subjective value of *not-G* given *not-A*. In addition to the preceding, there comes the subjective likelihood that P can do A, the subjective likelihood that P can refrain from doing A, and the exertion involved in doing A and in refraining from doing A. Although many of these can often be eliminated with some confidence, they re-enter the picture when the results of a study indicate a deviation from the expected results. In other words, these variables are always there although they may often be held constant at 1.00 or 0.00. The list of ten variables serves to call to attention the fact that a moral or other premium is often put on doing or refraining from doing something, regardless of the outcome. It is often better to have failed after trying than to have failed without trying. Furthermore, persons often lack the necessary confidence to carry out an act or, in some cases, to refrain from carrying it out. There may also be a positive premium on refraining from doing an act, regardless of outcome, and there may be a negative premium on trying and failing. Finally, nothing follows from the known subjective value of G about the subjective value of *not-G*, with or without having tried A. The effect of exertion on trying may be expressed in the following axiom:

Axiom 4.3.5 *P wants to minimize exertion.*

Note 4.3.6 This axiom does not state that people are lazy, but only that a want to minimize exertion exists among other wants. The extent to which it determines trying depends on the relative strengths of the entire set of wants and beliefs involved.

Corollary 4.3.7 **If P in C at t believes that he or she can perform either act A or act B and no other acts in order to reach G, and P's only want in C at t is to reach G, and P believes that A and B are equally likely to lead to G, and**

P believes that *A* involves less exertion than *B*, then *P* in *C* at *t* will try to perform *A*. Proof: this follows directly from Axiom 4.3.5.

Note 4.3.8 The deviations from the theoretical utility function observed in empirical research are generally open to reinterpretation. Frequently, many of the ten variables mentioned above are given only perfunctory attention. Furthermore, one seldom bothers to get estimates of all the *subjective* magnitudes of likelihoods and values.

Note 4.3.9 A series of derivations from Axiom 4.3.1 and Definition 4.3.2 are much less disputed than the general principle.

Corollary 4.3.10 **If *P*'s only want in *C* at *t* is to achieve *G*, and if *P* believes that trying to do *A* in *C* at *t* is the alternative with the highest likelihood of leading to *G*, if *P* believes that he or she can perform *A* in *C* at *t*, and if the alternative acts that *P* believes he or she can perform are believed by *P* not to involve less exertion than A, then *P* will try to do *A* in *C* at *t*.** Proof: since all other factors are excluded, the corollary follows directly from Axiom 4.3.1, which states that *P* wants to minimize exertion.

Theorem 4.3.11 **If in *C* at *t* there are available a number of action possibilities which *P* believes involve the same degree of exertion and have equiprobable outcomes, and if *P* believes that *A* leads to the outcome involving the highest pleasure, then *P* in *C* at *t* will try to do *A*.** Proof: according to Axiom 2.2.17, the strength of a want is directly proportional to the expected pleasure of fulfillment. Hence, *P*'s want to get the outcome of *A* is the strongest in *C* at *t*. But, according to Definition 2.1.14, *P* will act according to the strongest want. Therefore, the theorem follows.

Corollary 4.3.12 **If *P*'s only want in *C* at *t* is to achieve *G*, and if *P* tries to do *A* in *C* at *t*, and if no alternative act is believed by *P* to involve less exertion than *A*, then *P* believes that trying to do *A* is the alternative with the highest likelihood of leading to *G*.** Proof: this follows directly from Axiom 4.3.1.

Theorem 4.3.13 **If *P* believes that in *C* at *t* there are possible a number of actions with equiprobable outcomes and involving equal exertion, and if *P* tries to do *A* in *C* at *t*, then *A* is the alternative from which *P* expects the most pleasure.** Proof: since, in *C* at *t*, the alternatives are believed by *P* to involve equal exertion and to have equiprobable outcomes and since *P* tries to do *A*, it follows from Definition 2.1.14 that *P*'s want of the outcome of *A* is the strongest want of *P* in *C* at *t*. But from this it follows, by Axiom 2.2.17, that the outcome of *A* is the alternative from which *P* expects the most pleasure.

Note 4.3.14 Corollary 4.3.12 and Theorem 4.3.13 are among the most frequently used formulas for estimating the relative strength of a person's beliefs and wants in everyday life.

Corollary 4.3.15 **If *P* does not believe that he or she can do *A* in *C* at *t*, then *P* does not try** to do *A* in *C* at *t*. Proof: if *P* does not believe that he or she can do *A* in *C* at *t*, it follows that *P* does not believe that trying to do *A* in *C* at *t* will lead to the wanted outcome. But, from this and Axiom 4.3.1 it follows that *P* will not try to do *A* in *C* at *t*, and, hence, the corollary is proved.

Summary

An act is carried out only when the person can do it and tries to do it. A person can do an act only when the person's ability is higher than the difficulty of the act for that person. A person tries to do an act only when the person believes that this is the most useful act to do at that moment. By "useful" is meant here "likely to lead to pleasure" (fulfillment of wants). The three factors involved in the concept of useful are likelihood that trying to do something will lead to the goal, the exertion believed to be involved, and the subjective value of that goal. The likelihood that trying something will lead to a goal is composed of the likelihood that one will succeed in doing the act and the likelihood that the act will lead to the expected goal. The logic of action is the simplest and most developed part of psycho-logic.

5 Characteristics of Persons

Note 5.0.0 There exist a number of characteristics which are shared by all persons, by virtue of their being persons. This means that it is difficult to conceive of a person without these characteristics. To do so would require a change in the concept of person as developed here. Most of the characteristics to be described have to do with wants, but there are also some beliefs shared by all persons.

5.1 Wants

Note 5.1.0 It has already been pointed out that there are no limits to what a person could want. On the other hand, there are numerous wants that a person *must* have. Many of them are shared with animals. These are the ones having to do directly with the maintenance of the body and the species, such as hunger, thirst, sex, avoidance of extreme temperatures and pain, and so on. However, there are other wants which occur only in persons, and a few of these will be treated here. They have to do with *respect, care, understanding,* and *control.* Although one may find animal analogies, these tend to be incomplete.

5.2 Respect

Definition 5.2.0 **"P treats Q with respect"** = df **"P treats Q as someone having all the rights and duties that every person of the given status shall have."**

Note 5.2.1 By "status" is meant here "position in a social system." The given definition means that **P** treats **Q** courteously and justly, acknowledging **Q**'s societally defined rights and duties, and expecting **Q** to treat others, including **P,** according to correspondingly appropriate rules. Obviously, the specific rights and duties making up the concrete content of respect will vary from one culture to another. In contemporary Western societies, the right to have an autonomous private life, and the duty to accord this right to others is much emphasized, as is the basically egalitarian status of individuals.

Note 5.2.2 "Respect," as defined here, should not be confused with *admiration* for what someone has done, or *fear* of someone's powers. Admiration and fear are related to superiority in power and/or personal ability, whereas respect is related to position in a social system. A person is entitled to be treated with respect *merely* because he or she is a person with a particular status. To be treated without respect is to be denied that status and, thus, to be ignored as not being an accepted member of the society. To behave nonrespectably is to disregard one's duties as member of a society, with a particular status.

Theorem 5.2.3 **Every person wants to be treated with respect and wants to behave respectably.** Proof: according to Definition 5.2.0, not to be treated with respect is not to be treated as someone having all the rights and duties that every person of the given status shall have. But if the person shall have these rights and duties and if the person acknowledges the validity of this norm, then it follows from Axiom 2.5.5 that the person wants to be treated with respect and wants to behave respectably toward others. Hence, the theorem follows.

Note 5.2.4 It does not contradict the preceding that a person may not *want* to have a certain status and, hence, may *want* to escape the particular rights and duties linked with that status.

Note 5.2.5 If a person does not want to be treated with respect and does not want to behave respectably, then, according to Axiom 2.5.5, the person does not acknowledge the validity of the relevant norms and, hence, does not want to be a member of the community in which these norms are taken to be valid. However, there is *always* another, real or imagined, society, reference group, or reference person from whom the person wants to receive respect, and relative to whom the person *wants* to behave respectably. To behave respectably obviously also includes treating others with appropriate respect.

Note 5.2.6 To behave respectably is also to behave in a way "worthy of" respect. The underlying model is clearly that one "earns" respect, and that it is hard to treat someone with respect who does not reciprocate. On the other hand, there is a tendency to think that merely being a person with a given status entitles one to be treated with the appropriate respect. This dilemma is a recurrent one and cannot ever be definitely settled.

Note 5.2.7 Several feelings are closely linked to the occurrence or nonoccurrence of respect. A person who consistently behaves respectably and is treated with respect may experience the variant of happiness called *pride*. This feeling is noticeable only when there has been some deviation and/or some doubt and when, consequently, respectability is not entirely taken for granted. More specifically, pride will, then, arise when the person behaves respectably and accepts the corresponding norms as valid. The person may, obviously, behave in a manner that others regard as respectable and know this and, yet, feel no pride because he or she does not regard the corresponding norms as valid. Conversely, a person who treats someone else with disrespect may feel *guilty*. Specifically, this will occur if the person believes that he or she has behaved disrespectfully according to the norms accepted as valid by the other, and if he or she regards the other as a person. As we have seen in Chapter 3, disrespect is also the principal reason for *anger*. If *P* believes that he or she has been intentionally or inexcusably treated without respect, and if retaliation is not seen as impossible or too dangerous, then *P* will become angry. If *P* is ridiculed for not having behaved respectably, then *P* feels *ashamed*. If *P* is consistently treated without respect by persons important to *P*, and if the prospect of retaliating successfully and changing the situation appears hopeless, then the anger may change into *sadness*. Finally, if *P* has treated another person without respect and becomes aware of this, *P* will feel *guilty*. In general, many of the conflicts in human life stem from the deep-seated want to be respected and to respect others.

5.3 Care

Definition 5.3.0 **"*P* cares for *Q*"**= df **"*P* wants *Q* to be happy."**

Corollary 5.3.1 **If *P* cares for *Q*, then *P* wants to keep track of how things go with *Q*.** Proof: according to Definition 5.3.0, if *P* cares for *Q*, then *P* wants *Q* to be happy. But in order to know when something needs to be done to keep *Q* happy, *P* must keep track of how things go with *Q*.

Theorem 5.3.2 **If *P* cares for *Q*, then *P* tries to improve *Q*'s lot, unless other acts have a higher expected utility for *P*.** Proof: according to Definition 5.3.0, since *P* cares for *Q*, *P* wants to make *Q* happy. But, in order to make *Q* happy, *Q*'s lot must be improved. Since trying to improve *Q*'s lot is taken to have the highest expected utility for *P*, it follows from Axiom 4.3.1 that *P* will try to improve *Q*'s lot. Hence, the theorem is proved.

Theorem 5.3.3 **If *P* cares for *Q*, then *P* is satisfied when *Q* is happy.** Proof: according to Definition 5.3.0, if *P* cares for *Q*, then *P* wants *Q* to be happy. But, according to Definition 2.2.23, when a want is fulfilled there is an increment in pleasure. Hence, the theorem follows.

Theorem 5.3.4 **If *P* cares for *Q*, then *P* is dissatisfied when *Q* is unhappy.** Proof: according to Definition 5.3.0, if *P* cares for *Q*, then *P* wants *Q* to be happy. But, according to Definition 2.2.24, when a want is not fulfilled there is decrement in pleasure. Hence, the theorem follows.

Definition 5.3.5 *"P likes Q"* = df *"P wants to be with Q."*

Note 5.3.6 "Care" should not be confused with liking a person, although they, normally, go together. You may like to be with a person because you think the person is beautiful, sexy, funny, a good listener, entertaining, because he or she likes, understands or cares for *you,* and so on. However, "like" may refer to personal pleasure only. On the other hand, care involves concern about the other person's situation and, hence, is an *altruistic* want. The distinction between liking because one derives pleasure from being with a person and care about that person becomes clear when the person no longer provides pleasure. When the beautiful person gets fat or wrinkled, when the entertainer gets angry, the liking linked only to personal pleasure may diminish, whereas the care, if there is any, will remain.

Axiom 5.3.7 **Every person wants to be cared for by someone and wants to care for someone.**

Note 5.3.8 The preceding proposition has been given the status of axiom because the last part of it appears hard to prove within the given system. However, the first part may be proved as follows: Q either cares for P, is indifferent toward P, or is hostile toward P. If Q is indifferent toward P, then Q will do nothing to make P happy or to prevent P from becoming unhappy. Since P knows this and since P wants to be happy and to avoid being unhappy, P must want Q not to be indifferent. Similarly, if Q is hostile toward P, then Q will try to make P unhappy. Since P knows this and since P wants to be happy and to avoid being unhappy, P must want Q not to be hostile. It follows from the preceding that P must want Q to care for P.

Note 5.3.9 The frequent occurrence of persons living more or less without any caring relationships need not be taken to weaken the plausibility of Axiom 5.3.7. First, one may want to escape from isolation without being able to do so. In order to try, there must be no other want or combination of wants stronger than the want to be cared for and care for. We know that there is often such a stronger want, for example, to avoid being rejected and ridiculed. Secondly, even if the fear of rejection is overcome, and the person tries to get out of the isolation, this may fail because of external circumstances (task difficulty) and/or because of lack of ability (social skill).

Note 5.3.10 The widespread practice of keeping pets is consistent with Axiom 5.3.7. People may care deeply for pets and often also believe that the pets care for them.

Note 5.3.11 The sentiment of *liking* a person, defined as wanting to be *with* a person (Definition 5.3.5), also involves a fundamental striving toward reciprocity which may be expressed as follows:

Theorem 5.3.12 **P wants his or her liking of a person to be reciprocated.** Proof: according to Definition 5.3.5, *P*'s liking *Q* means *P* wants to be with *Q*. But, *P* knows that the likelihood of achieving this goal is sharply increased if *Q* likes *P* and, hence, wants to be with *P*. This follows because persons try to achieve what they want. Hence, it follows that *P* will want *Q* to want to be with *P*, that is, according to Definition 5.3.5, *P* will want *Q* to like *P*.

5.4 *Understanding*

Definition 5.4.0 *"P understands what Q means by saying or doing A"*= df *"P and Q agree as to (a) what is equivalent to A; (b) what is implied by A; (c) what is denied by A; and (d) what is irrelevant to A."*

Note 5.4.1 Since the set of expressions consisting of what is equivalent to, implied by, denied by, and irrelevant to a given expression is infinite in size, understanding of what was meant can never be ascertained completely and with certainty. Usually, understanding is only ascertained as far as it has immediate practical consequences.

Definition 5.4.2 *"P understands why Q does A"*= df *"P and Q agree about which wants and beliefs of Q were involved in Q doing A."*

Note 5.4.3 Definitions 5.4.0 and 5.4.2 concern, respectively, understanding of what is meant by an expression (act) and of what led to an expression (act). The first is understanding of what follows from something, and the second is understanding of what something follows from.

Note 5.4.4 Understanding of what is expressed and of why it is expressed should not be confused with agreement in beliefs or agreement on values. There is mutual understanding between *P* and *Q* when they agree on what is equivalent, and so on, to the given expression, *A*, and on what beliefs and wants led to the act *A*. However, it does not follow from this mutual understanding that they agree about *A*'s truth or about *A*'s value. Understanding is a precondition for, but not identical to, agreement or disagreement about facts or values. Without understanding, the possibility of pseudoagreement and pseudodisagreement is imminent.

Theorem 5.4.5 **Every person wants to be understood by others and wants to understand others.** Proof: if a person does not understand others and is not understood by them, no orderly interaction can occur. This follows because without understanding there is no agreement about what is meant by acts and about why they are performed (Definitions 5.4.0 and 5.4.2). Hence, the participants cannot anticipate each other's future actions. But, in order to achieve goals involving interaction with others, the

59

person must be able to anticipate their actions, and they must be able to anticipate his or hers. Therefore, it follows that the person must want to understand and be understood.

Note 5.4.6 The preceding theorem is *one* way in which the want to understand and to be understood can be proved within the present system. It is equally fundamental as the corresponding theorem about respect (5.2.3) and axiom about care (5.3.6). All three could have been given the status of axioms.

Note 5.4.7 It does not follow from Theorem 5.4.5 that everyone *always* tries to make him- or herself understood and tries to understand others. In accordance with Axiom 4.3.1, trying only occurs under conditions of maximal expected utility. This means that trying to make oneself intelligible and to understand others is restricted to those situations where it appears to be advantageous. Under many conditions, other wants, such as fear, shame, and so on, may be stronger than the want to understand and be understood.

Theorem 5.4.8 **Every person wants to understand him- or herself.** Proof: if a person does not understand him- or herself, no orderly planning of behavior can occur. But, in order to achieve any goals, the person must be able to anticipate own behavior under various circumstances. Therefore, the person must want to understand him- or herself. (The theorem may also be deduced from Axiom 2.4.2, stating that P wants to believe what is the case.)

Note 5.4.9 The notion of self-understanding can be clearly subsumed under Definitions 5.4.0 and 5.4.2. One understands what one's expressions mean to the extent that one knows what they are equivalent to, and so on. Similarly, one understands one's acts to the extent that one knows what wants and beliefs they stem from. Clearly, this applies only to reflective understanding. Unreflectively, a person must, usually, understand him- or herself. This follows from Axiom 1.5.0, which asserts that awareness and action tend to be completely integrated. A person functions according to an almost unitary system of what is taken for granted.

Note 5.4.10 Since people frequently do not try to unveil themselves to others and frequently do not try to understand others and since, according to Theorem 5.4.5, they want to be understood and to understand others, it follows that there must be powerful contrary wants. Some of these are obvious. You want to avoid being punished, ridiculed, rejected, ignored, abused, and so on. Revealing yourself makes you more vulnerable and easier to manipulate. If the other person is malevolent, he or she may use the information about you to cause you pain and harm. This may be formulated as follows:

Theorem 5.4.11 **If *P* believes that *Q* does not care for *P*, then *P* will try not to give *Q* information which may be used by *Q* to cause *P* harm or pain.** Proof: if *Q* does not care for *P*, *Q* must either be indifferent or hostile to *P*. If *Q* is indifferent, this means that *Q* may harm *P* through lack of interest in avoiding the indifference and also through not protecting *P*. If *Q* is hostile to *P*, *Q* is likely to try to harm *P*. In both cases, it follows that, since *P* wants to avoid harm (pain), *P* will try to withhold information from *Q*.

Note 5.4.12 The reason why people often do not try to understand others, even when this is directly relevant for a project at hand, may be that such understanding could give them guilt feelings (in situations where the question is, "who is guilty?"), or could threaten their plans and feelings of autonomy (in situations where the question is, "who is in charge?"). Another reason is that trying to understand involves exertion, and people want to minimize exertion (Axiom 4.3.5).

Note 5.4.13 Understanding is a necessary condition for a person to function. If a person encounters totally incomprehensible others and is himself or herself totally unintelligible to these others, no orderly interaction can ensue. The only solution is a rapid socialization process in which the participants acquire a set of shared meanings.

5.5 *Control*

Definition 5.5.0 *"P controls E"* = df *"P can make E occur and not occur according to his or her wants."*

Note 5.5.1 The concept of control is linked here to the concept of want. You have control over that which can be made to vary according to your wants. Two other closely related terms are *"power"* and *"freedom."* "Power" is another term for "can." Instead of saying, *"P can do A"* one may say, *"P has the power to do A."* "Freedom" is a term which (a) emphasizes certain aspects which I think are less important in the present context; (b) has a smaller field of application than "control"; and (c) may lead to certain unfruitful controversies. Let me elaborate on these points. First, "freedom" emphasizes that one can *choose* what to do, whereas "control" emphasizes the link between want and result. But what is most important to a person is usually not the *choice* as such, but the fact that he or she can satisfy his or her wants. Secondly, people mostly live and act unreflectively, and at this level of awareness it makes no sense to talk about freedom and choice. You don't *choose* to turn on the light switch or to slice bread with your right instead of your left hand. The alternatives are not psychologically real. What is important is that, when you want it, you get light and slices of bread. Thirdly, freedom as a phenomenon only exists at the level of reflective awareness. But here one encounters the unending debate about freedom of will. This debate is unending because one cannot agree on criteria for deciding for and against. On the other hand, it is, in principle, clear how to decide whether or not one has control over an event, see Definition 5.5.0. For the preceding reasons the term "control" has been preferred here.

Theorem 5.5.2 **Every person wants to have control in matters involving the fulfillment of personal wants.** Proof: according to Definition 5.5.0, control enables a person to fulfill his or her wants. Therefore, every person must want to have control in matters involving the fulfillment of such wants.

Note 5.5.3 The term "personal want" is used to distinguish wants which are linked to the individual person from wants which have to do with obeying norms taken to be valid for everyone, cf. Note 2.5.0 and Axiom 2.5.5. These latter wants may be labeled *"normative."*

Theorem 5.5.4 **Every person wants to have control in matters involving norms taken by that person to be valid.** Proof: according to Axiom 2.5.5, persons want to obey norms they take to be valid. Hence, they want to have control in order to ensure their own obedience.

Note 5.5.5 If the person believes that she or he does not have sufficient control, she or he may ask for help in resisting temptation, apply for commitment to an institution, and so on. The theorem may also be said to state that persons wish to satisfy their personal wants in a respectable way, that is, in a way which does not conflict with existing norms. There are three types of control:

Definition 5.5.6 *"P in C at t has own-control of act A"* = df *"P in C at t can do or not do A according to his or her wants, independently of the wants of other persons."*

Note 5.5.7 This is a situation in which **P** can say, "You cannot stop me from doing it," "You cannot force me to do it." The term "own-control" is a little awkward, but together with the two other terms to be introduced, it makes clear sense and covers an important distinction in everyday life.

Definition 5.5.8 *"P in C at t has other-control of Q's act A"* = df *"P in C at t can make Q do or not do A, according to P's wants, independently of Q's wants."*

Note 5.5.9 In this situation **P** can say, "I decide what you do and don't do," "I can make you do it," "I can stop you from doing it." Again, there is a mild neologism, "other-control," which should be easy to understand and which corresponds clearly to a distinction made in everyday life.

Definition 5.5.10 *"P in C at t has self-control of act A"* = df *"P in C at t does or does not*

> do *A* according to his or her normative wants and not according to his or her personal wants when these are in conflict."

Note 5.5.11   This means that the person with self-control acts according to what he or she regards as *right,* even when this conflicts with what he or she wants personally.

Note 5.5.12   There are three main problems of control in every person's life. One is the balance between *P*'s own-control and other persons' control of *P*. At the one extreme is the completely independent person who can prevent others from influencing him or her in any way. At the other extreme is the completely dependent person who has no internal steering. The second problem is the balance between *P*'s other-control and the other person's own-control. At the one extreme is the powerful person who can direct other persons' behavior in every detail. At the other extreme is the totally powerless person who cannot in any way interfere with others' behavior. Finally, the third problem is the balance between *P*'s normative and *P*'s personal wants and beliefs. At the one extreme is the totally controlled person who never does anything he or she considers to be wrong. At the other extreme is the totally uncontrolled person who lives only according to his or her momentary personal wants and is incapable of restraint.

Note 5.5.13   How can lack of self-control be understood in terms of the present system? It represents a deviation from the normal state of integration formulated in Axiom 1.5.0 and involves the performance of acts which the person him- or herself regards as *wrong.* A clue is found in the fact that lack of self-control presupposes awareness *that* there is a discrepancy, in other words, a state of reflective awareness (Definition 1.3.0). According to Axiom 1.3.4, this means that the person can *describe* the lack of self-control, that is, the fact that he or she does something he or she does not want to do and does not do what he or she wants to do. It follows from Axiom 4.3.1 and Definition 4.3.2 that, for the person involved, the wrong act has a higher expected utility than the correct act. But, this means that the person must be acting according to wants and beliefs other than those described by the person as the correct ones. In other words, the *context* of acting, that is, what is taken into account in acting (Definition 1.5.5), must be different. It is common knowledge that when there is lack of self-control, the person's context for acting is temporally *narrower* than that involved in the person's reflective awareness. The person is a victim of the here-and-now, his or her momentary impressions, temptations, and impulses. What is known about long-term consequences is not taken into account. Among such consequences are being held responsible for one's actions, and, hence, the person's actions are often described as "irresponsible."

63

Note 5.5.14 Logically, there are eight possible extreme states of control or lack of control which may characterize a person's situation at a given time and in a given context.

State 1 **High own-control, high other-control, high self-control.** This may be a powerful, domineering person who functions well, and/or a person in a superordinate position who functions well.

State 2 **High own-control, high other-control, low self-control.** This may be a powerful, domineering person and/or a person in a superordinate position who functions irresponsibly in the here-and-now.

State 3 **High own-control, low other-control, high self-control.** This describes a situation in which a well-functioning person can do what he or she likes, but has no control of what the other one does. An example could be cooperation between officials in two independent government institutions, no one having any authority over the other.

State 4 **High own-control, low other-control, low self-control.** This is a situation in which a person functions irresponsibly in the here-and-now, not letting others interfere, and incapable of interfering with what others do.

State 5 **Low own-control, high other-control, high self-control.** This exemplifies a situation in which a well-functioning person is cooperating on equal footing with others. Each person is dependent on the others, and decisions can only be made through negotiated agreement. Each person can veto any decision.

State 6 **Low own-control, high other-control, low self-control.** Mutual dependence of persons who function irresponsibly in the here-and-now. This is bound to become a chaotic and violent scenario.

State 7 **Low own-control, low other-control, high self-control.** This could be a case of a well-functioning, but powerless, person, perhaps in a very subordinate position.

State 8 **Low own-control, low other-control, low self-control.** This would be a weak person, or a person in a subordinate position, functioning irresponsibly in the here-and-now.

Note 5.5.15 Persons with high self-control are said to function well. This means that they act according to what they think is right. High self-control should not be confused with compulsive restraint of all spontaneity. High self-control is compatible with a high degree of spontaneity in situations judged to be appropriate for this, in the context of the total life situation. Hence, high self-control involves maximal flexibility. Compulsivity is a sign of *low* self-control. The compulsive person cannot let go, that is, act in the here-and-now, even when he or she regards this as the right thing to do. Compulsivity involves automatic, unreflective control. It should be noted that there is no paradox of the type "be spontaneous" involved here. One can decide to *relinquish* control, but what one does *after* that is not a matter of reflective decision.

Note 5.5.16   The eight possible extreme states that a person may be in may be reduced to three types of extreme dyadic relations between persons who have high or low self-control. The first type is the master-slave or superordinate-subordinate relation, the second is the cooperation of mutually dependent partners, and the third is the cooperation of mutually independent partners. The superordinate person has high own-control and high other-control, and the subordinate person has correspondingly low own-control and low other-control. Both mutually dependent partners have low own-control and high other-control, each can stop the other from doing something. The mutually independent partners both have high own-control and low other-control. These cannot control each other. It is common to the two last combinations that they can act together only when both agree.

5.6 Beliefs About Existence

Note 5.6.0   As was already pointed out in Note 2.3.1, there is, in principle, no limit to what a person could believe. There are, nevertheless, certain beliefs common to all persons and *only* to persons. Some of these will be described here.

Axiom 5.6.1   **Every person reflectively believes that he or she exists.**

Note 5.6.2   Everyone takes him- or herself unreflectively for granted. This is especially clear in anticipating outcomes of interactive situations in which one is involved and in which one's own impact influences events. However, persons also reflectively believe that they *exist* as an entity. The distinction between the "I" and the "me" is implicit in the concept of reflectivity, as are also the distinctions between the "I" and the "it," and the "I" and the "you." The firm belief in one's own existence as an entity is hard to analyze since there is no clearly delimited reference object. The body is clearly different from the person, not only as witnessed by the multiple personalities, but also by the meaningfulness and ease of talking about dreams or near-dying experiences of being outside and observing one's own body. What is referred to as "me" is the experienced unity behind all the concrete manifestations of the person. This is also often referred to as the "soul."

Corollary 5.6.3   **Every person reflectively believes in the possibility of his or her nonexistence.** Proof: this follows directly from Axiom 5.6.1. The reflective awareness *that* one exists means that there is awareness of the possibility of nonexistence, that is, death.

Note 5.6.4   Reflective awareness of the empirical certainty of eventual death apparently alternates with a kind of unreflective taking for granted of one's immortality.

Axiom 5.6.5 **Every person wants to continue to exist.**

Note 5.6.6 Although the want to continue to exist is one of the strongest that people have, it is sometimes weaker than the want to escape from the suffering of life. In line with the general distinction between unreflective and reflective acting, one may, roughly, distinguish between spontaneous and premeditated suicide attempts. The spontaneous suicide attempt occurs when the person is overwhelmed by accumulated suffering and acts spontaneously in a here-and-now context. The premeditated suicide attempt is planned over time and involves reflective awareness in the context of the person's total life situation. Obviously, many suicide attempts may involve intermediate or mixed states of awareness.

Corollary 5.6.7 **If a person attempts suicide, then that person has a want to escape suffering, which is stronger than the want to continue to live.** Proof: according to Axiom 5.6.5, every person wants to continue to exist. But, since the person tries to cease to exist, it follows, from Corollary 2.1.20, that the want to cease to exist is stronger than the want to continue living. Hence, the corollary follows.

Note 5.6.8 It is apparent that people's existential problems are closely linked with religious concerns. Life is sacred whereas the present concept of strength of motive is profane, hence, the slightly jarring tone of the proof of Corollary 5.6.7. It is also apparent that the possibilities of achieving eternal life and the conditions of this future life are almost always linked with *moral* considerations, that is, with the way in which the person acts relative to the norm-system of the given culture. Sinners are generally condemned to death, hell, or otherwise impoverished conditions in future existences (reincarnation).

5.7 Beliefs About a Shared Conceptual System of Psychology

Note 5.7.0 There remains a set of beliefs common to all persons which has to do with their taking for granted that what they see as necessary conceptual relationships are also seen as such by everyone else. In order to characterize these beliefs, some definitions are needed.

Definition 5.7.1 **"A psychological proposition"** = df **"A proposition about something which exists for persons."**

Note 5.7.2 Evidently all propositions in the present system are psychological and so are all other propositions dealing with the awareness and activity of persons, including their abilities, wants, beliefs, feelings, and acts.

Definition 5.7.3 **"A valid psychological proposition"** = df **"A psychological proposition taken to be necessarily true by all persons."**

Note 5.7.4 The validity of a psychological proposition can be checked through asking a sample of informants to judge its correctness and the correctness of its negation. If everyone agrees that the proposition as formulated must necessarily be correct, and that its negation could not conceivably be correct, this strengthens the assumption that the proposition is valid. This procedure could, conceivably, be applied to the present system of propositions, and, given that the methods were adequate, could constitute a check on its validity.

Note 5.7.5 The propositions to be set forth all have to do with what persons take for granted about the shared nature of valid psychological propositions. They will be given status as axioms, since they cannot be proved within the present system.

Axiom 5.7.6 **For every valid psychological proposition X, there exists a valid psychological proposition Y, where $Y=$ "Every person takes it for granted that X is valid for every person."**

Note 5.7.7 The preceding axiom states that if everyone regards a psychological proposition as necessarily correct, then everyone takes it for granted that the proposition also applies to everyone else.

Axiom 5.7.8 **For every valid psychological proposition X, there exists a valid psychological proposition Z, where $Z=$ "Every person takes it for granted that every person takes it for granted that X is valid for every person."**

Note 5.7.9 The preceding axiom states that if everyone regards a psychological proposition as necessarily correct, then everyone takes it for granted that everyone else also takes it for granted that the proposition applies to everyone.

Axiom 5.7.10 **For every valid psychological proposition X, there exists a valid psychological proposition V, where $V=$ "Every person takes it for granted that every person takes it for granted that every other person also takes it for granted that the proposition X applies to every person."**

Note 5.7.11 The preceding axiom states that if everyone regards a psychological proposition as necessarily correct, then everyone takes it for granted that everyone else also takes it for granted that everyone else takes it for granted that the proposition applies to everyone.

Note 5.7.12 It follows from the preceding that every single valid proposition included in the present system corresponds to three other valid propositions, which enhances the power and applicability of the system threefold. In order to illustrate the three highly abstract axioms, let X be equal to Theorem 5.2.3 which reads: *Every person wants to be treated with respect and wants to behave respectably.* By applying each of the three axioms given above to this theorem, we arrive at the following three new theorems:

Theorem 5.7.13 (5.2.3 a) **Every person takes it for granted that every person wants to be treated with respect and wants to behave respectably.** Proof: this follows directly from Theorem 5.2.3 and Axiom 5.7.6.

Theorem 5.7.14 (5.2.3 b) **Every person takes it for granted that every person takes it for granted that every person wants to be treated with respect and wants to behave respectably.** Proof: this follows directly from Theorem 5.2.3 and Axiom 5.7.8.

Theorem 5.7.15 (5.2.3 c) **Every person takes it for granted that every person takes it for granted that every person takes it for granted that every person wants to be treated with respect and wants to behave respectably.** Proof: this follows directly from Theorem 5.2.3 and Axiom 5.7.10.

Note 5.7.16 The mirror-hall effect of Axioms 5.7.6, 5.7.8, and 5.7.10 enhances the predictability of behavior tremendously. Not only do the axioms facilitate the prediction of individual behavior, but they also enable us to predict complex interactions of many people under the simplifying assumption that everyone assumes that everyone else masters the common conceptual psychological system. Some aspects of this will be treated in Chapter 7.

Summary

A number of characteristics, notably wants and beliefs, are shared by all persons by virtue of their being persons. Persons share a number of wants with animals, such as hunger, thirst, sex, avoidance of pain, and so on. However, there are also some wants which occur only in persons. These include the want to be treated with *respect* and to behave *respectably* toward others, the want to be *cared* for and to *care* for someone, the want to be *understood* by others and to *understand* them, the want to *control* others and to be *controlled* by them. Persons also uniformly believe in their own *existence* and in the *existence* of other persons. Finally, persons believe that all persons share the complete system of valid psychological propositions, that is, commonsense psychology.

6 Personal Change

Note 6.0.0 Changes occur all the time in what a person wants, believes, feels, and does. These changes are, in principle, ambiguous in that they may reflect either a higher or a lower level dispositional change in the person or merely a change in the momentary external or internal circumstances influencing the person. When a former scoundrel starts behaving respectably, the question is always, has he or she really changed for the better or is it merely dissemblance for some shady purpose. In order to deal with this type of question, one may distinguish roughly between *first-order* and *second-order* changes.

6.1 Types of Change

Definition 6.1.0 **"First-order change" = df "A change in what a person is aware of and/or does, which does not involve a change in any disposition."**

Note 6.1.1 First-order changes are strictly reversible. Given the question, "What day is it today?", *P* answers "Tuesday," and, when asked the same question the next day, answers "Wednesday." This change in acting is a strictly reversible first-order change which does not indicate any change of the person, but only in the external circumstances. One week later, the person again answers "Tuesday." Another example: given the question "Are you hungry?", *P* answers "yes." *P* then has dinner and upon being given the same question now answers "no." This change too is strictly reversible and does not indicate that the person has changed. When asked the same question five hours later, the person again answers "yes." However, there are also first-order changes reflecting irreversible external or internal changes. Given the question, "Has the last train left?", the person answers "no." A little later, and from then on, the person answers "yes" to the same question. Similarly, given the question, "Do you read without glasses?", the person answers "yes," but, some years later, and from then on, answers "no" to the same question. First-order changes are not intrinsically stable dispositional changes, but reflect changes in the circumstances surrounding the person. In principle, they can be reversed, if the external circumstances are reversed. If it turns out that the last train has not left after all, or if the person, after an operation, regains his or her ability to read without glasses, the acting will be correspondingly reversed. First-order changes are part of the process of keeping track of the actual situation.

Definition 6.1.2 **"Second-order change" = df "Change in a person's dispositions for becoming aware of and for acting."**

Note 6.1.3 A disposition has the general form "if X then Y" and is stable over a period of time. If the person *always,* when there is an X-type situation, displays a Y-type awareness and/or acting, then we infer a disposition. Dispositions make up what is orderly and predictable about a person in any given time period. They indicate what is constant during the flux of first-order changes. The following example is intended to show how a second-order change is a change in the repeated pattern of first-order changes. A rebellious young person has for years always tried to cross streets at the red light and to wait at the green light. This is a stable pattern of first-order changes – stop walking on green, start walking on red – and, hence, indicates a disposition. In the process of coming of age, the person changes to become a law-abiding citizen. From now on, he or she stops at the red light and crosses at green. There is now a new pattern of first-order changes, and, therefore, the disposition has changed. This is a second-order change. Actual cases of change always involve ambiguity. Suppose that the street light sequences are all part of a film and that the young person is played by an actor according to a script. In this case, the actor is not changing as a person, but is merely displaying first-order changes. This is clearly shown when the director is dissatisfied with the effect, and everything has to be retaken.

Note 6.1.4 A crucial difference between first- and second-order changes is that the former are always reversible whereas the latter are always irreversible. The person who can no longer read without glasses may, through a revolutionary medical technique, regain this ability and will again answer "yes" to the question "Can you read without glasses?". On the other hand, second-order changes involving discrimination and differentiation are irreversible. This is formulated in the following axiom:

Axiom 6.1.5 **Discrimination and differentiation are irreversible.**

Note 6.1.6 If a person becomes aware of a difference between D_1 and D_2 (discrimination) and/or if a person becomes able to distinguish in actual performance between two ways of action, A_1 and A_2 (differentiation), there is no direct way of making the person unaware of these differences again. One cannot undiscriminate or undifferentiate. This is one

of the fundamental principles of psychology. Another principle underlying personal change may be formulated as follows:

Axiom 6.1.7 **A person's awareness of the future consists of extrapolations from that person's awareness of trends in the past.**

Note 6.1.8 "Extrapolation" means that a given trend is taken to continue. Given no other relevant information, an unchanging trend is expected to remain unchanged, increasing or decreasing trends are expected to con-
tinue, positively or negatively accelerated trends are expected to con-
tinue, and so on. This does not mean that one cannot anticipate unique and new events. If current trends continue, one may, for example, anticipate that they will reach critical values, lead to catastro-
phies, and so on. Such anticipations are based on *combinations* of complex previous information. However, basically, *P*'s only guideline to the future is that it will be a continuation of trends in the past.

Note 6.1.9 Axiom 6.1.7 means that changes based on experience are to some ex-
tent irreversible. The past cannot be entirely undone or ignored. Every repetition has previous occasions as part of its background (context). When a psychologist's client regains a long-lost trust in people, the new trust differs from the original in that it has the intermediate peri-
od of mistrust as context. The effect of previous experience cannot be completely wiped out, but only masked or overlaid with the outcome of new experience. Changes resulting from experience have two aspects. Insofar as experience simply leads to expectancy of what is followed by what or what leads to what and involves a recombination of already existing categories of awareness and action, the resulting change is reversible. On the other hand, to the extent that the experience has led to the development of discriminations and differentia-
tions, its outcome is irreversible. The transition from unreflective to reflective is also irreversible. If you have become reflectively aware of something you can never again become merely unreflectively aware of it. The irreversibility may also be expressed by saying that there is no process of becoming unreflective. The reader is reminded that "unreflective" means that the person *cannot* talk about something (Ax-
iom 1.3.4). Hence, if you have once become able to talk about some-
thing, you cannot again become unable to do this, even though the relevant performance may become automatic.

Corollary 6.1.10 **Learning to predict future events does not occur on the basis of trends in what "actually" happens, but on the basis of what *P* is aware of.** Proof: this follows directly from Axiom 6.1.7.

Note 6.1.11 This corollary means that the lessons of experience are often hard to anticipate. There may be highly regular patterns in what happens to or around a person, yet nothing is learned if the person is not aware of

71

them. On the other hand, the fast and exceedingly complex socialization of children into a culture can take place only because they are provided with "precooked" experience, prepared in an easily recognizable and, therefore, learnable form.

Note 6.1.12 The basic types of dispositions organizing a person's awareness and actions may be labeled *"knowledge"* and *"preference."* Knowledge manifested in awareness is called *"belief"* (know-that), and knowledge manifested in the way acts are carried out is called *"skill"* (know-how). Preference manifested in awareness is called *"want,"* and preference manifested in how action is carried out is called *"style"* (preferred ways of acting). At the level of elementary acts these cannot be differentiated. An act may indicate belief, skill, want, and style at the same time. However, these are clearly conceptually distinct. In a two-choice situation, an act indicates strength of belief only, if the outcomes of the alternatives are equally preferable, if the alternatives are equally difficult, and if they can be executed in only one way. The same act indicates want only if the outcome of the alternatives is equiprobable, if the alternatives are equally difficult, and if they can be executed in only one way. In a two-choice situation where the alternatives are equally difficult and differ only in *how* they are executed, and where the value and likelihood of the outcome are constant, differences in performance indicate differences in preferred style. Finally, in a two-choice situation in which value and likelihood of outcome are constant and only one way of executing the act is possible, whereas the difficulty of execution varies, differences in acting indicate differences in skill.

Note 6.1.13 The preceding may be summarized as follows: isolated changes in acting are ambiguous. They may be adjustments to changes in the momentary situation (first-order) or changes in dispositions (second-order). Second-order changes are reversible insofar as they involve changes in expectancy of what is followed by what or what leads to what. Second-order changes are irreversible insofar as they involve discriminations or differentiations or a transition from unreflective to reflective.

6.2 Open and Closed Systems

Note 6.2.0 The outcome of personal change may take the form of *open* or *closed* systems of beliefs and wants. A closed system is characterized by allowing only first-order, reversible changes. It can incorporate or reject every sort of information and cannot be changed by any counterevidence. If the system includes the dispositional belief "if X then Y," and *"X and not-Y"* is observed, then this is taken to be evidence not that "if X then Y" is wrong, but that either X or Y is not really the case. A classical, intensely studied example of closed systems is the concept of conservation. If a person has achieved such a concept and is then shown an apparent falsification (two equally heavy balls of plasticine, one ball deformed into a sausage, ball is now heavier than sausage, as indicated on a pair of scales) the notion is typically not given up. Instead the person will argue that something is the matter with the scales used for measuring weight, that something has been lost on the floor or has stuck to the hand, that the experimenter has cheated, and so on. The concept of conservation, insofar as it is taken to be self-evident, is not at stake. Similar closed systems can easily be found in people's views of moral, political, religious, and other matters. A person's conception of self and others is, typically, a closed system which can incorporate almost any event without changing. In psychotherapy, the task is often to try to open up seemingly completely closed systems.

Note 6.2.1 Open systems are, in principle, vulnerable to experience and imagination and, hence, admit genuine dispositional change. Three theorems are central in this connection:

Theorem 6.2.2 **If P is aware of and takes it to be relevant that X is sometimes followed by Y and sometimes followed by Z, and that both Y and Z occur only after X, then P will want to find and try out indices of type a in X, such that a is always followed by Y and $-a$ is always followed by Z.** Proof: without having found an index of type a, P's belief about what will happen after X will often be erroneous. Since, according to Axiom 2.4.2, P wants to believe what is the case, it follows that P will want to find an index of type a which will make this possible.

Note 6.2.3 It should be mentioned that a is a part or an aspect of X, or a combination of parts or aspects of X. Theorem 6.2.2 describes what may be labeled a "want to find *relevant differentiating cues*." Whether or not a person will actually search for such cues in a given situation at a given time obviously depends on the relative strength of other wants and beliefs active at that time.

Theorem 6.2.4 **If P is aware of and takes it to be relevant that X is always followed by Z and Y is always followed by Z and Z occurs only after X or Y, then P will want to find and try out indices of type b, common to X and Y, such that b is always followed by Z and $-b$ is always followed by *not-Z*.** Proof: since having two hypotheses and two explanations involves more exertion than having only one hypothesis and one explanation, and since P wants to avoid exertion (Axiom 4.3.5), it follows that P will want to find ways to simplify the prediction and explanation of Z.

Note 6.2.5 It is taken for granted that prediction from or to a disjunctive concept involves more cognitive effort than prediction to or from a conjunctive concept. Theorem 6.2.4 describes a want to find a *relevant common factor*. Whether or not a person will actually search for such a factor in a given situation at a given time will, obviously, depend on the relative strength of the other wants and beliefs active at that time.

Theorem 6.2.6 **If *P* is aware of and takes it to be relevant that a member of category *X* is followed by a member of category *Y*, and no other information, taken by *P* to be relevant, is available, then *P* will tentatively believe that a new member of *X* will be followed by a new member of *Y*.** Proof: according to Axiom 6.1.7, *P*'s awareness of the future consists of extrapolations from *P*'s awareness of trends in the past. *P* is aware of a trend in the past where an *X* is followed by a *Y*. Since no other information is assumed to be available to *P*, it follows from Axiom 6.1.7 that *P* will expect another *X* to be followed by another *Y*.

Note 6.2.7 Theorem 6.2.6 describes what may be labeled the "principle that *equals are expected to be followed by equals.*" This is another very basic psychological principle.

Note 6.2.8 Given that there exists a set *X* and a set *Y* such that a member of *X* is always followed by a member of *Y*, and given that *P* searches for such a combination of sets, the probability that *P* will find it is dependent on the probability that *P* will notice that an *X* is actually followed by a *Y*. In practice, one always tries to optimalize the conditions for learning through increasing the *salience* of the relevant events. The term "salience" refers to the likelihood that something will be recognized. The perceptual conditions of recognition include such factors as size, intensity, movement against a stationary background, and, most efficiently, the direct pointing out of the relevant events or features. It should be added, however, that the mere sequencing of salient events does not necessarily lead to an expectancy that there is a regularity. Such expectancies are profoundly influenced by the person's already existing conception of the world, or, in the case of infants, by their genetically determined predispositions. Note the highly variable difficulties in conditioning responses to different kinds of stimuli. From everyday adult life, one example should suffice. A person spills coffee on the floor and, immediately after that, the siren of an ambulance is heard. Both events are very salient and the person is clearly aware of them. Nevertheless, no expectancy is formed that spilling coffee on the floor will bring forth the sound of an ambulance. The reason is clearly that this does not fit into the person's view of the causal structure of the world.

Note 6.2.9 An important variant of a closed system is what is commonly called a *"mental problem,"* which involves unadaptive behavior and, hence, makes life more difficult. The origin and form of such a problem may be as follows: P in C_l at t_l does A and this is followed by a painful event G, or P simply encounters C_l at t_l and this is followed by G. According to Axiom 6.1.7, P will come to expect that doing A in C or merely encountering C will be followed by the painful event G. But, according to Definition 2.2.2, P will want to avoid the pain and, therefore, according to Axiom 4.3.1, will try to avoid it in ways most likely to succeed. This avoidance of doing A in C, or of C, may be regarded as a mental problem under the following circumstances:

Definition 6.2.10 **"P has a mental problem"** = df **"P tries to avoid and escape from any action or context of type X, even though P knows reflectively that contexts of this type are not generally followed by pain, and this way of acting creates difficulties in P's life that are considered serious by P and/or by persons interacting with P."**

Note 6.2.11 Stable mental problems indicate maladaptive closed systems. A task of psychotherapy is to open such systems up so that they can change.

Note 6.2.12 Mental problems may also become apparent through various *symptoms*. A few of these may be mentioned here. If P is very *afraid* without any apparent reason, this may mean that something unreflectively feared is present or imminent. If P is very *depressed*, it may mean that there are so many contexts to be avoided, that important goals have become apparently unattainable. Obviously, depression may also reflect unattainability as such, without any intermediary fear. If P behaves in very stereotyped and restricted ways (compulsively), it may mean that these are narrow pathways between areas to be avoided.

Note 6.2.13 The distinctions between first- and second-order changes and between open and closed systems are gradual rather than dichotomous. There are many intermediary changes which are hard to classify clearly as first- or second-order, and there are systems which are only relatively open or closed. However, there are also easily reversible momentary adjustments which cannot be said to involve changes in the person's dispositions. At the other extreme, there are discriminations and differentiations which change the person's repertory for ever and can never be undone. In view of the preceding discussion, it should be clear that the task of differentiating between first- and second-order change is very complicated indeed. It is also fairly clear that currently popular measures of therapeutic effect, such as changes in response to questionnaires and inventories, which are extremely susceptible to instructional and other context effects, must be regarded as relatively useless. Only evidence that a person is now capable of making discriminations and differentiations which he or she *could not* make earlier should be taken as evidence of genuine therapeutic change. Other changes should most naturally be interpreted as reflecting the continuing interaction between client and therapist. By this is meant that responses to research instruments presented after a therapy should be seen as possibly reflecting the client's responses to the therapist and to self, in the context of a preceding more or less prolonged and expensive interaction.

6.3 Changes in Acting

Note 6.3.0 Procedures aimed at changing a person may be directed primarily at abilities, want, beliefs, feelings, or acts. However, since these are not conceptually unrelated, every procedure will tend to involve several or all of them. Since acting always involves all five categories, the conditions of change of acting will be considered first. Later, procedures specifically directed at changing abilities, wants, beliefs, and feelings can be singled out.

Corollary 6.3.1 **P changes from doing A in C at t_1 to not doing A in C at t_2 if, and only if, there is a change from "P can do A in C at t_1" to "P cannot do A in C at t_2" and/or a change from "P tries to do A in C at t_1" to "P does not try to do A in C at t_2."** Proof: this follows directly from Axiom 4.1.0.

Corollary 6.3.2 **P changes from not doing A in C at t_1 to doing A in C at t_2 if, and only if, there is a change from "P cannot do A in C at t_1" to "P can do A in C at t_2" and/or a change from "P does not try to do A in C at t_1" to "P tries to do A in C at t_2."** Proof: this follows directly from Axiom 4.1.0.

Note 6.3.3 A change in acting in the same context always means a change in can or a change in trying or a change in both can and trying. The next step is to formulate separately the conditions for a change in can and in trying.

6.4 Changes in Can

Corollary 6.4.0 **There is a change from "P can do A in C at t_1" to "P cannot do A in C at t_2" if, and only if, (a) P's ability to do A in C has decreased from t_1 to t_2; and/or (b) the difficulty for P of A in C has increased from t_1 to t_2, the net effect of (a) and (b) being a change from P's ability to do A in C at t_1 being greater than the difficulty for P of A in C at t_1 to P's ability to do A in C at t_2 being smaller than the difficulty for P of A in C at t_2.** Proof: this follows directly from Axiom 4.2.0.

Corollary 6.4.1 **There is a change from "P cannot do A in C at t_1" to "P can do A in C at t_2" if, and only if, (a) P's ability to do A in C has increased from t_1 to t_2; and/or (b) the difficulty for P of A in C has decreased from t_1 to t_2, the net effect of (a) and (b) being a change from P's ability to do A in C at t_1 being lower than the difficulty for P of A in C at t_1 to P's ability to do A**

in C at t_2 being higher than the difficulty for P of A in C at t_2. Proof: this follows directly from Axiom 4.2.0.

Corollary 6.4.2 **The effect of any increment or decrement in the ability of P to do A in C can be compensated by a corresponding increment or decrement in the difficulty for P of A in C and vice versa.** Proof: this follows directly from Axiom 4.2.0.

Note 6.4.3 The preceding three corollaries expressing the effect of changes in ability and difficulty on can are used routinely in everyday life. The present system contains no principles determining changes in ability and difficulty. However, it is apparent that a detailed analysis of the components of specific abilities and difficulties will enable one to predict what learning and what situational changes will lead to required behavioral changes. The next step is to formulate the effects of component variables on changes in trying.

6.5 Changes in Trying

Corollary 6.5.0 **There is a change from P in C at t_1 trying to do A in order to achieve G, to P in C at t_2 not trying to do A in order to achieve G if, and only if, the expected utility of trying to do A in order to achieve G changes from t_1 to t_2 from being the highest to not being the highest for P in C.** Proof: this follows directly from Axiom 4.3.1.

Corollary 6.5.1 **There is a change from P in C at t_1 not trying to do A in order to achieve G to P in C at t_2 trying to do A in order to achieve G if, and only if, the expected utility of trying to do A in order to achieve G changes from t_1 to t_2 from not being to being the highest for P in C.** Proof: this follows directly from Axiom 4.3.1.

Note 6.5.2 Since changes in expected utility can come about through changes in strength of the relevant wants or in strength of the relevant beliefs, or in both, a couple of more specific corollaries may be derived from Axiom 4.3.1.

Corollary 6.5.3 **If there is a change from P in C at t_1 trying to do A in order to achieve G to P in C at t_2 not trying to do A in order to achieve G, then (a) P's want to achieve G has declined in strength relative to P's other wants; and/or (b) P's belief that trying to do A leads to G has declined in strength relative to P's other beliefs relevant to achieving G.** Proof: this follows directly from Axiom 4.3.1 and the definition of expected utility (4.3.2).

Corollary 6.5.4 **If there is a change from P in C at t_1 not trying to do A in order to achieve G to P in C at t_2 trying to do A in order to achieve G, then (a) P's want to achieve G has increased in strength relative to P's other wants; and/or (b) P's belief that trying to do A leads to G has increased in** strength relative to *P*'s other beliefs relevant to achieving *G*. Proof: this follows directly from Axiom 4.3.1 and the definition of expected utility (4.3.2).

6.6 Changes in Determinants of Trying

Note 6.6.0 Although the main determinant of trying, expected utility, is the product of only two variables, namely strength of want and strength of belief, each of these is the result of two components. Strength of want is equal to the strength of the want to reach the goal, minus the strength of the want to avoid exertion. Hence, the strength of the want to reach a goal varies according to the strenuousness of the alternative means of reaching that goal. (This analysis can also be applied to the interesting special case where the main goal is precisely to exert oneself because it is believed to be healthy.) Similarly, the strength of the belief that trying to do a certain act will lead to the goal is the result of two factors, namely the strength of the belief that the person can perform the act and the strength of the belief that the act leads to the goal. Hence, the strength of the belief that trying to do the act will lead to the goal is the *product* of the strength of the belief that the person can successfully perform the act and the strength of the belief that the act leads to the goal. These four factors are, in turn, the outcomes of certain antecedents and, hence, yield the following formal propositions involving changes in the determinants of trying:

Corollary 6.6.1 **P's want in C to reach G rather than H is strengthened from t_1 to t_2 if the increment in pleasure (decrement in pain) expected by P in C to result from achieving G rather than H is increased from t_1 to t_2.** Proof: this follows directly from Axiom 2.2.17.

Corollary 6.6.2 **P's want in C to reach G rather than H is weakened from t_1 to t_2 if the increment in pleasure (decrement in pain) expected by P in C to result from achieving G rather than H is decreased from t_1 to t_2.** Proof: this follows directly from Axiom 2.2.17.

Corollary 6.6.3 **P's want in C to try to do A rather than B in order to reach G is strengthened from t_1 to t_2 if the expected strenuousness of doing A compared to doing B is decreased from t_1 to t_2.** Proof: this follows directly from Axiom 4.3.4.

Corollary 6.6.4 **P's want in C to try to do A rather than B in order to reach G is weakened from t_1 to t_2 if the expected strenuousness of doing A compared to doing B is increased from t_1 to t_2.** Proof: this follows directly from Axiom 4.3.4.

Note 6.6.5 By the strength of *P*'s want to reach *G* rather than *H* and to do *A* rather than B is meant the *relative* strength of the first want compared to the second want. Similarly, the expected increment in pleasure and the expected strenuousness is the *relative* expected increment in pleasure and the *relative* strenuousness compared to the alternative or alternatives.

Note 6.6.6   Corollaries 6.6.3 and 6.6.4 evidently do not apply in the special case where the main goal is to maximize strenuousness (because this is seen as healthy).

Corollary 6.6.7   **P's belief in C that A leads to G is strengthened from t_1 to t_2 if, and only if, the likelihood for P in C that A leads to G is increased from t_1 to t_2.** Proof: this follows directly from Axiom 2.3.20.

Corollary 6.6.8   **P's belief in C that A leads to G is weakened from t_1 to t_2 if, and only if, the likelihood for P in C that A leads to G is decreased from t_1 to t_2.** Proof: this follows directly from Axiom 2.3.20.

Corollary 6.6.9   **P's belief in C that P can perform A is strengthened from t_1 to t_2 if, and only if, the likelihood for P in C that P can perform A is increased from t_1 to t_2.** Proof: this follows directly from Axiom 2.3.20.

Corollary 6.6.10   **P's belief in C that P can perform A is weakened from t_1 to t_2 if, and only if, the likelihood for P in C that P can perform A is decreased from t_1 to t_2.** Proof: this follows directly from Axiom 2.3.20.

Note 6.6.11   The preceding eight corollaries formulate procedures for changing the likelihood that P in C will try to perform A in order to reach G. All of them involve changes in expectancy. The basic condition for such changes is expressed in Axiom 6.1.7, stating that expectancy about the future relies on an extrapolation from trends in the past. In order to change expectancy, the person must be given credible information supporting a change. Such information may either take the form of actual experiences, arranged in such a salient way that the person is likely to notice them, or through indirect information, either oral or written, but presented by persons or sources which are highly credible to P. "Credible" of course means that their communications are likely to be believed.

6.7 Change of Feeling

Note 6.7.0   Since feelings are not conceptually independent of wants and beliefs, changes in feelings involve the same factors as changes in wants and beliefs. Even so, formulations directly concerning feelings may be helpful for particular purposes. First, there follows a general proposition about feelings.

Corollary 6.7.1 **P's feeling in C changes if, and only if, either P's relevant wants change, with P's relevant beliefs constant; or P's relevant beliefs change, with P's relevant wants constant; or both P's relevant wants and P's relevant beliefs change, but in such a way that these changes do not exactly compensate each other.** Proof: this follows directly from Definition 3.1.1 which states that feelings are defined by the relationship between a person's wants and beliefs.

Note 6.7.2 The formulation of Corollary 6.7.1 states that, in order for a feeling to change, the changes in wants and beliefs must not exactly compensate each other. Example: the want to escape a danger diminishes, hence diminishing the fear, but the likelihood of the feared event increases hence increasing the fear. If the decrement and increment are exactly equal, the outcome is an unchanged degree of fear, even though both the relevant want and the relevant belief has changed.

Note 6.7.3 The preceding means that changing wants and/or beliefs exhausts the possibilities for changing feelings. If someone takes Valium to reduce fear and if there is no change in the person's relevant beliefs, then it follows that Valium must have changed (weakened) the want of the person (to escape the danger). Conversely, if there is no change in the want of the person to escape the danger, then Valium must have changed the person's estimate of the likelihood that what is feared will actually happen. Finally, the present analysis denies the possibility that Valium reduces fear while leaving unchanged both the want and the belief of the person, or the relationship between these.

Note 6.7.4 As has been pointed out earlier, amount of physiological arousal is a symptom of feeling, but not a criterion. If a person has a high degree of arousal, but does not have any want to escape a painful event and does not believe that such an event is possible, then the arousal cannot be labeled "fear." In practice, high arousal may be taken as a symptom that the person harbors a strong feeling. However, *what* this feeling is must be decided by considering what wants and beliefs are involved. Also, since arousal is a symptom and not a criterion, it is conceivable that a person is in a state of strong arousal for some *other* reason than having a feeling. Conversely, it is conceivable that a person has a strong feeling even though not being strongly aroused physiologically.

Note 6.7.5 Although nothing more can be said generally about changing feelings, it is possible to formulate a set of corollaries, two for each of the ten feelings included in the present system. One corollary for each feeling states how that feeling is created and the other states how the feeling is erased. Although these corollaries may appear to add little, given the definitions of the feelings, they nevertheless serve as summaries of the explanations that are given in everyday life of the creation and erasing of feelings.

Corollary 6.7.6 **If P comes to believe that one of P's wants is being, or is going to be, fulfilled, then P becomes happy.** Proof: this follows directly from Definition 3.4.2.

Note 6.7.7 This corollary also incorporates the case where *P* is given something which is not wanted in advance, but which creates pleasure. This makes *P* want to retain it, and the fulfillment of this newly created want creates pleasure.

Corollary 6.7.8 **If P comes to believe that one of P's wants is being, or is going to be, frustrated, then P becomes unhappy.** Proof: this follows directly from Definition 3.4.2.

Note 6.7.9 This corollary also incorporates the case where *P* is given something which *P* has not wanted to avoid in advance, but which creates pain. This makes *P* want to avoid it, and the lack of fulfillment of this want means unhappiness.

Corollary 6.7.10 **If P in C at t comes to believe that he or she cannot fulfill or act toward a future fulfillment of any want in C, that C is not, for P, the occasion for any other want, and that P cannot leave C for some time, then P becomes bored.** Proof: this follows directly from Definition 3.5.2.

Corollary 6.7.11 **If P in C at t is bored and then comes to believe that he or she can fulfill or act toward a future fulfillment of at least one want in C, and/or that C, for P, is the occasion for at least one want, and/or that P may leave C at any time, then P will cease to be bored.** Proof: this follows directly from Definition 3.5.2.

Corollary 6.7.12 **If P comes to believe that he or she has intentionally or through indefensible thoughtlessness been treated without consideration (without respect), then P becomes angry and wants to retaliate.** Proof: this follows directly from Definition 3.5.5.

Corollary 6.7.13 **If P is angry and P then comes to believe that he or she has not intentionally or through indefensible thoughtlessness been treated without consideration (without respect), then P ceases to be angry and ceases to want to retaliate.** Proof: this follows directly from Definition 3.5.5.

Corollary 6.7.14 **If P in C at t comes to believe that, regardless of what he or she does, there is a definite probability that he or she will be hurt (will experience pain), then P becomes afraid.** Proof: this follows directly from Definition 3.5.12.

Corollary 6.7.15 **If P in C at t is afraid and then comes to believe that it is improbable that he or she will be hurt, regardless of what he or she does, then P will cease to be afraid.** Proof: this follows directly from Definition 3.5.12.

Corollary 6.7.16 **If P in C at t comes to believe that he or she has been observed doing something which ought not to be done in public, either because it is not** regarded as seemly or because it is done incompetently, then *P* becomes ashamed. Proof: this follows directly from Definition 3.5.16.

Corollary 6.7.17 If *P* in *C* at *t* is ashamed and then comes to believe that he or she has not been observed doing anything which ought not to be done in public, either because it is not regarded as seemly or because it is done incompetently, then *P* ceases to be ashamed. Proof: this follows directly from Definition 3.5.16.

Corollary 6.7.18 If *P* in *C* at *t* comes to believe that he or she has done something wrong to someone, then *P* begins to feel guilty. Proof: this follows directly from Definition 3.5.19.

Corollary 6.7.19 If *P* in *C* at *t* is feeling guilty and then comes to believe that he or she has not done anything wrong to anyone, then *P* ceases to feel guilty. Proof: this follows directly from Definition 3.5.19.

Note 6.7.20 Corollary 6.7.19 does not describe the only way in which a person may cease to feel guilty, cf. Note 3.5.22.

Corollary 6.7.21 If *P* in *C* at *t* comes to believe that something he or she wants to attain has become, and will remain, forever unattainable or something which he or she has wanted to keep has become irrevocably lost, *P* will become sad. Proof: this follows directly from Definition 3.5.23.

Corollary 6.7.22 If *P* in *C* at *t* is sad about losing something and then comes to believe that this something has not become, or will not remain forever, unattainable or has not become irrevocably lost, then *P* will cease to be sad. Proof: this follows directly from Definition 3.5.23.

Corollary 6.7.23 If *P* in *C* at *t* comes to believe that his or her lot in life can never be improved in the way he or she wants it to be, or he or she can never become the sort of person he or she wants to be, then *P* will become depressed. Proof: this follows directly from Definition 3.5.26.

Corollary 6.7.24 If *P* in *C* at *t* is depressed and then comes to believe that his or her lot in life can be improved in the way he or she wants it, and/or he or she can become the sort of person he or she wants to be, then *P* will cease to be depressed. Proof: this follows directly from Definition 3.5.26.

Corollary 6.7.25 If *P* in *C* at *t* begins to want to have what *Q* has and to want *Q* not to have it, then *P* is becoming envious of *Q*. Proof: this follows directly from Definition 3.5.29.

Corollary 6.7.26 If *P* in *C* at *t* is envious of *Q* and then ceases to want to have what *Q* has and to want *Q* not to have it, then *P* ceases to be envious of *Q*. Proof: this follows directly from Definition 3.5.29.

Corollary 6.7.27 If *P* in *C* at *t* comes to believe that something may not be what it seems to be and wants to know what it is, then *P* is becoming suspicious. Proof: this follows directly from Definition 3.5.31.

Corollary 6.7.28 **If P in C at t is suspicious about something and then comes to believe that this something is what it seems to be, then P will cease to be suspicious about it.** Proof: this follows directly from Definition 3.5.31.

Corollary 6.7.29 **If P in C at t comes into contact with something, and contact with this something is incompatible with P's moral and/or esthetic and/or hygienic standards, then P becomes disgusted.** Proof: this follows directly from Definition 3.5.34.

Corollary 6.7.30 **If P in C at t is disgusted by being in contact with something and then ceases to be in contact with this something, then P ceases to be disgusted.** Proof: this follows directly from Definition 3.5.34.

Note 6.7.31 This is not the only way in which P may cease to be disgusted. Obviously, this may also occur if P's standards were to change.

6.8 Changes in Subjective Identity

Note 6.8.0 In all the preceding examples, P is treated as a constant. Frome one point of view, P is simply the organized system consisting of P's abilities, preferences, beliefs, wants, norms, skills, styles, and feelings. According to this, P changes every time one of the components changes. However, this does not take into account the distinction that can be made between changes in what a person *actually* can do, wants, prefers, believes, and so on, and changes in what the person takes for granted about him- or herself. One example of this is the person who gradually became very competent in his or her job, but who continued to behave *as if* he or she were basically incompetent. The explanation of this is that what he or she took for granted about him- or herself formed the background for all the experiences of success. Hence, when this person succeeded in something, it was automatically interpreted as the accidental or insignificant success of an incompetent person. The incompetence was taken for granted and, hence, determined how outcomes were interpreted in such a way that successes could have no influence on the self-image. The conditions for a change in unreflective subjective identity, protected by all-encompassing presuppositions remain to be explicated.

Summary

Changes in a person may be subdivided into first-order changes, which simply reflect changes in the surrounding context, and second-order changes, which are changes in the person's dispositions. First-order changes are strictly reversible and so are second-order changes involving learning what follows after what, and what leads to what. On the other hand, second-order changes involving discrimination between situations and differentiation between acts, and transition from the unreflective to the reflective mode are strictly irreversible. The basic principle of learning is that a person's awareness of the future is based on extrapolations from the past as it was experienced by that person. Under special conditions, there is an automatic search for relevant differentiating cues or for relevant common factors. Changes in acting depend systematically on changes in can and try. Changes in can depend on changes in the ability of the person and the difficulty of the task, and changes in try depend on changes in want, likelihood of achieving the outcome, and likelihood of being able to carry out the act involved. Changes in feelings occur only as a function of changes in the constituent wants and beliefs. Finally, subjective identity may remain unchanged even when actual performance changes radically.

7 Interacting

Note 7.0.0 Only the *triad* has sufficient complexity to incorporate all the basic aspects of human interaction. A main reason for this is that much of what people do involves communication to someone *about* a third person. The realization of this is expressed in the prototype example described in the Introduction, p.3. The indispensability in everyday life, not only of first- and second-, but also of third-person formulations in descriptions of what goes on between people also illustrates this very well. The triad becomes automatically incorporated in the present system when this is fully expanded into the set of "mirror propositions" described in Chapter 5, p.67. The "mirroring" means that every person believes that every other person believes that every person believes in the commonsense propositions of the present system. For a triad of persons, *A, B,* and *C,* this means that, for example, *A* believes that *B* believes that *C* believes in each valid commonsense proposition, and so on. This has definite consequences for the description, explanation, and prediction of the interaction of any group of three persons. In spite of what has been said programmatically above, only two-person interactions will be treated in this chapter. The main reason for this is that these are more elementary and more easily accessible intuitively. The rough conceptual apparatus developed here needs to be consolidated and refined before it can be used to face the complexity of groups of three or more persons.

7.1 Some Elementary General Concepts

Definition 7.1.0 *"P and Q are interacting at t"* = df *"P, in acting at t, takes Q's earlier and future acts into account, and Q, in acting at t, takes P's earlier and future acts into account, and the goals of both P and Q include changes in the acting of the other person."*

Note 7.1.1 If something is to be regarded as an interaction, both participants must act in a way showing that the other one's acts make an actual or potential difference, and that their own acts are intended to make a difference in the other one's acts. Interaction is specified with respect to time, although *t* here refers to a time period rather than a moment. Context is not included in the definition since the participants never act in identical contexts and since the relative amount of shared context may vary over a wide range. However, for a complete characterization, the individual contexts of *P* and *Q* and their overlap should be specified.

Theorem 7.1.2 **If *P* and *Q* are interacting during *t*, then *P* and *Q* are aware of each other's acts and take them to be relevant for their projects at hand.** Proof: according to Definition 7.1.0, interaction means that each interactant takes into account the other one's acts. According to Definition 1.2.13, taking *O* into account means that changes in *O* make a difference, directly or indirectly, in the way the person acts. But, according to Theorem 1.2.16, if a change in *O* makes a difference in a person's acting, then that person is aware of *O* and takes *O* to be relevant for his or her projects at hand. Hence, the theorem follows.

Note 7.1.3 Since interaction involves awareness, it may be more or less reflective. In face-to-face interaction, the mutual adjustments in posture, facial expression, intonation, and so on, are so complicated and occur so rapidly that they cannot be monitored reflectively. In the slow interaction involved in written correspondence, reflectiveness has optimal conditions.

Note 7.1.4 In most human interaction *talking* plays a major role and needs to be distinguished from other action. In what follows, verbal acts will be referred to as "says" or "said," and nonverbal acts as "does" or "did." In contexts were action in general is the topic, "does" and "did" will still be used to refer both to verbal and nonverbal acting. A fundamental precondition for any ordered interaction is the presence of some degree of understanding in each of two somewhat different senses:

Definition 7.1.5 (Identical to Definition 5.4.0) **"*P* understands what *Q* means by saying or doing *A*"** = df **"*P* and *Q* agree about (a) what is equivalent to *A*; (b) what is implied by *A*; (c) what is denied by *A*; and (d) what is irrelevant to *A*."**

Definition 7.1.6 (Identical to Definition 5.4.2) **"*P* understands why *Q* does *a*"** = df **"*P* and *Q* agree about which wants and beliefs of *Q* were involved in *Q* doing *A*."**

Note 7.1.7 The two definitions cover both *what* an act means and *why* it was carried out. Agreement is emphasized as the criterion of understanding in both cases. Since *Q* was the actor, he or she is normally regarded as authority on what was meant by his or her act and on why it was carried out. Hence, if there is no agreement, there is misunderstanding, and it is *P* who misunderstands *Q*. This is another example of the basic principle that a person defines his or her own experiences, in this case what he or she means and intends. The only precondition for this is that the person is honest when making the description and experiences it as adequate.

Note 7.1.8 At any moment in an interaction process, each participant may believe reflectively or take for granted unreflectively that there is agreement, that is, understanding, or may suspect reflectively or unreflectively that there is no agreement and, hence, misunderstanding. The more suspicious a participant is with respect to whether he or she and/or the other one understands adequately, the more frequently and persistently will he or she check on this. Typically, checking occurs through producing exemplars of expressions believed to be equivalent, implied by, negated by, or irrelevant to the given one and observing the resulting overt agreement or disagreement.

Note 7.1.9 When one of the participants is an alleged expert, (for example, a psychologist) he or she may claim to understand a person's acts better than the person understands him- or herself. In this case, the criterion of understanding is not agreement, but ability to predict the person's acting, feelings, and so on. This concept involves understanding another person's *unreflective* processes.

Note 7.1.10 It is apparent that some degree of mutual understanding is necessary for orderly interaction to occur. However, it is also clear that, in order to determine the degree of understanding that exists, it is necessary to presuppose mutual understanding, at least of some terms or expressions indicating equivalence, implication, contradiction, and irrelevance, as well as true and false, yes and no, and so on. Without shared understanding of these, the participants cannot even know whether they agree or not. This is also another example of the more general principle that there can be no understanding without preunderstanding.

Definition 7.1.11 **"*P* and *Q* are having a conversation"** = df **"*P* and *Q* are talking to each other and listening to each other and have at least some mutual understanding."**

Definition 7.1.12 **"*Q* is talking to *P*"** = df **"*Q* is talking with a want to be understood by *P*."**

Definition 7.1.13 **"*Q* is listening to *P*"** = df **"*Q* is listening with a want to understand what *P* says."**

Note 7.1.14 Understanding is clearly a matter of degree. There is almost never a total lack of understanding and there is almost never a perfect understanding. In everyday life there is usually sufficient understanding to ensure the orderly progress of societal life, see also 5.4.0–5.4.13.

7.2 Taxonomy of Two-Person Interactions in Terms of the Control Concept

Note 7.2.0 Own-control and other-control of a given act, in a two-person interaction, are linked by definition (5.5.6 and 5.5.8). In a group of two persons, *P* and *Q*, if *P* has high own-control with respect to act *A*, then it follows that *Q* has low other-control with respect to *A*, and if *P* has high other-control with respect to *A*, then it follows that *Q* has low own-control with respect to *A*. Given this constraint, there are only three types of orderly two-person interactions. These will be labeled *"cooperation," "consultation,"* and *"coercion."*

Definition 7.2.1 **"*P* and *Q* are cooperating with respect to *A*"** = df **"*P* and *Q* are interacting and both have low own-control and high other-control with respect to *A*."**

Note 7.2.2 In cooperation, as defined here, no one can act without the other one agreeing. The joint project is carried out on the basis of negotiated agreements in which each participant can veto every proposed action. Obviously, this is an ideal type. In reality, partners are seldom absolutely equal in negotiating and vetoing power.

Note 7.2.3 Every interaction process is nested within a hierarchy of processes. Hence, what at a given level appears to be an instance of cooperation may occur within the context of one person *forcing* the other to cooperate. Hence, seen within a wider context, an instance of cooperation may turn out to be an instance of coercion. In some cases, the opposite is the case. An instance of coercion may result from an agreement originating in a consulting situation or a cooperating situation. *P* promises to be wholly obedient to *Q* within a given context, yet the promise itself was given in a situation totally without coercion.

Definition 7.2.4 **"*P* and *Q* are consulting with respect to *A*"** = df **"*P* and *Q* are interacting and both have high own-control and low other-control with respect to *A*."**

Note 7.2.5 In consultation, as defined here, no one can force the other one to do or not do *A*. Much human interaction, in the form of conversations, belongs to this type. There may be no commitment to a common project, but merely an exchange of information relevant for such projects as the participants may be interested in.

Definition 7.2.6 **"*P* is coercing *Q* with respect to *A*"** = df **"*P* and *Q* are interacting, and *P* has high own-control and high other-control with respect to *A*, whereas *Q* has low own-control and low other-control with respect to *A*."**

Note 7.2.7 In coercion, as defined here, *P* can get *Q* to do or not do *A*, according to *P*'s wants, and *Q* cannot get *P* to do or not do *A* according to *Q*'s wants. This is a master-servant relationship in which everything occurs according to the master's wants.

Note 7.2.8 In all three cases of orderly interaction, there may occur a transition to a state of *conflict*. The transition occurs when **P** and **Q** come to regard their wants as incompatible. This means that the fulfillment of **P**'s wants excludes the fullfilment of **Q**'s wants and vice versa. It should be emphasized that conflicts are always defined by *beliefs* about incompatibility, rather than by *actual* incompatibility.

Definition 7.2.9 **"P and Q are in conflict with respect to X"** = df **"P and Q are interacting, and interaction according to P's wants and beliefs with respect to X is believed by both of the interactants to be incompatible with interaction according to Q's wants and beliefs, and vice versa."**

Note 7.2.10 A possible taxonomy of interpersonal conflicts may contain the following criteria: one is between conflicts based on unrealistic beliefs and conflicts based on realistic beliefs. The former group can be potentially solved through correction of inadequate beliefs, which may not be as easy in practice as it is in principle. The latter group has to be resolved through some kind of compromise. The realistic interpersonal conflicts may be divided into those where the participants want different things and have to get the same, and those where the participants want the same thing and have to get different things. A conflict about where to place a piece of furniture may illustrate the first type, and a conflict about who shall live in a given room may illustrate the second type. Obviously, many conflicts are settled through the use of force, which essentially means that cooperation and consultation are changed into coercion, or that a former coercive relationship is reversed.

7.3 Cases of Interaction

Note 7.3.0 In what follows, a few cases of interaction will be analyzed in order to determine if the system developed so far is sufficient to account for the expectable outcomes.

Case 7.3.1 **P and Q are having a conversation. P is happy and Q is bored. P overtly expresses his or her happiness, and Q, therefore, believes that P is happy being with Q. Q is bored being with P, but hides this. Hence, P believes that Q is happy too. No other wants and beliefs, and, hence, feelings of P and Q intervene.** According to Definition 3.4.2, happiness is based on a belief that a want is being, or is going to be, fulfilled. According to Definition 2.2.0, pleasure is what persons want to achieve, to maintain, and to increase. Hence, happiness is the feeling connected with the achievement and presence of pleasure. From this it follows that, since **P** is happy being with **Q**, **P** wants to continue being with **Q** and does not want **Q** to leave. On the other hand, since **Q** is bored being with *P* and since it follows from Definition 3.5.2 that persons want to avoid and escape from boring contexts, it follows that *Q* wants either to change the conversation into an interesting (= not boring) one, or to leave the company of *P*. If *Q* has tried and given up trying to make the conversation interesting from his or her point of view, then it only remains for *Q* to try to leave. According to Axiom 2.5.1, persons are expected always to account for their actions in acceptable ways, either explicitly or implicitly. Hence, *Q* is expected to account for his or her leaving the company of *P*. *Q* wants to leave *P* because he or she is bored. However, knowing commonsense psychology, *Q* believes that if he or she were to tell *P* about being bored, *P* would be hurt in a four-fold way. First, since *Q* believes that *P* is happy being with *Q*, it follows that *Q* believes that *P* will become frustrated and unhappy if *Q* leaves. Secondly, according to Theorem 5.3.12, everyone wants his or her liking of a person to be reciprocated. Since *Q* knows this, it follows that *Q* believes that expressing the boredom would hurt *P* because it would make it clear to *P* that *Q* does not like *P* as much as *P* likes *Q*. Thirdly, according to Axiom 5.3.6, every person wants to be cared for. Since *Q* knows this, it follows that *Q* believes that *P* would become unhappy if *Q* didn't bother to hide his or her boredom. This would indicate to *P* that *Q* does not want *P* to be happy, in other words, does not care for *P*. Finally, according to Theorem 5.2.3, every person wants to be treated with respect. Hence, *Q* knows that if *Q* does not hide the truth, *P* will feel treated in a rude and disrespectful way, which is painful. It would make *P* angry too (Definition 3.5.5).

It follows from the preceding that, since it is wrong to hurt someone, unless it is unavoidable in order to fulfill some obligation of an even higher order, *Q* will avoid telling *P* about being bored. It could be added that if *Q* had done that, not only would *Q*'s relationship with *P* become strained, but *Q* might become known to everyone as a heartless and/or tactless person. Hence, it is a very safe prediction that, in the given situation, *Q* will not tell *P* about his or her real reason for leaving. This prediction follows from the principles of the present system. However, as was already pointed out, it follows from Axiom 2.5.1 that *Q* must give *some* account of why he or she is leaving the company of *P*. Knowing commonsense psychology, *Q* will not refer to other personal wants, that is, something he or she *wants* to do. The reason for this is that reference to other personal wants involves a risk of *belittling Q*'s want to be with *P*. This follows because, since *Q* is leaving, the want to leave must be stronger than the want to stay (Definition 2.1.14). It also means that if *Q* expresses no doubt about wanting to leave, *Q*'s want to be with *P* must be *clearly* weaker than that other want. In fact, *P* may well come to suspect that *Q*'s want to be with him or her may be very weak indeed. This will be very painful too since, as already pointed out, *P* wants his or her liking of *Q* to be reciprocated

(Theorem 5.3.12). In view of these complications, Q is likely to avoid all reference to personal wants.

There remain only two categories of excuses which Q may use to account for his or her leaving. One of them involves *compelling circumstances,* such as a strong headache, being tired or unwell, having to catch a bus, and so on. Common to these circumstances are that they detract from any pleasure Q could derive from being with P and that they mean that Q would be in pain or severely inconvenienced. They are also intelligible to P and do not in any way hurt P. The other category of excuses involves *obligations* of some sort. Obligations have to be fulfilled by every respectable person, and P could not be assumed to want Q to behave unrespectably, that is, not to keep an appointment or a promise, not to uphold a commitment, and so on. Hence, Q can refer either to some invented compelling circumstances or some invented obligations, and leave, while expressing *regret* at not being able to stay, hence implying that, personally, Q really wants to stay with P. In order for this to work, Q must act convincingly, and the excuse should be plausible and difficult to check. However, even if P suspects the truth, P cannot inquire further into this, because this would be disrespectful and imply that Q could be dishonest. The outcome is that P will be left alone, but having been treated with care and respect during the process. Q will have escaped boredom, but has also behaved respectably and avoided feeling guilty from having hurt someone unnecessarily. On the other hand, a moral issue remains, namely the fact that Q has been dishonest. For some people this may create guilt and, hence, further complications. For others the norm not to hurt anyone, if it can be avoided, takes clear precedence over the norm to speak the truth, the whole truth, and nothing but the truth.

Case 7.3.2 **Quarreling. P and Q at t are having a conversation. P and Q are angry at each other.** Since P and Q are angry at each other, it follows from Definition 3.5.5 that they both must believe that the other has intentionally or thoughtlessly treated them without consideration (respect) and that they both want to undo this (retaliate). However, this means that they both blame each other for behaving in an unacceptable (unrespectful) way and, hence, for being guilty. Since, according to Definition 3.5.19, feeling guilty means feeling that one has done something wrong to someone, and since this involves a transgression of norms held to be valid, then, according to Axiom 2.5.5, both participants will want not to do or to have done this. It follows that both will try to deny that they are guilty and assert that the other one, or someone else, is guilty, or that circumstances beyond control are responsible. When accusations are restricted to the participants, there is some regularity in the interaction, which can be labeled a *"quarrel."* The quarrel is unpleasant since both participants are constantly accusing each other of being guilty and since the goal of getting even is never materialized. What are the options available to each participant?

1. Staying in the situation, accusing the other one of being the villain and presenting oneself as the saintly innocent victim or as the justifiably enraged and unforgiving victim. This ensures the continuation of the quarrel with a possible escalation toward some peak. The other one, receiving massive doses of blame, can hardly escape retaliating by returning the blame, and so on. The process is fired by the unspoken premise that either one or the other of the participants is to blame and by the painfulness of accepting guilt. The escalation follows from the premise that one cannot repeat literally what has already been said, to de-escalate means not freeing oneself completely of the blame and may sound like defeat, and, hence, the only option appears to be to escalate.

2. Leaving the situation, accusing the other one of being the villain and presenting oneself as the saintly innocent victim or as the justifiably enraged and unforgiving victim. This postpones the outcome and opens the possibility that everything will calm down, and/or that other matters will come to occupy the participants. On the other hand, the leaving also involves a fixation of the bad atmosphere and may also be seen as additional insult ("You are not worth talking to").

3. Another variant is to start to *cry,* hence ceasing one's direct accusations and presenting oneself as being merely a poor victim. This is an invitation to compassion and for the other one to regret his or her harsh words and deeds. It is very difficult for the other one to break through this and continue to accuse and blame. You don't kick one who is lying down. It can be done only by redefining the crying as being insincere and completely unjustified. Much depends on whether the crying is perceived as involving a continued accusation ("look how you are treating me"), or an acknowledgement of guilt ("I am so sorry for what I have done") or an invitation to lay down arms ("how stupid we are, both of us").

4. Taking the blame, asking forgiveness, ceasing to attribute guilt to the other one. This may be done honestly or may only be a pretense. If it is a pretense, it may be seen through and, hence, be of no avail. If it is honest, it will mean that the other one achieves his or her goal and ceases to be angry. Frequently, this will be followed by a similar admission on the part of the other person. "After all, we both have some guilt, the blame must be shared." or at least, the other one is forgiving and the good relationship is re-established. This strategy presupposes some tolerance for accepting guilt on one's own part. Presumably, such a tolerance can only be displayed by persons who have a strongly positive self-image, permitting them to allow the recognition of some faults. Persons with a strongly negative self-image with respect to some characteristic will not engage in quarrels involving that char-

acteristic simply because this creates no additional guilt. A professional thief need not be enraged by the accusation "You steal things." The
strategy of admitting guilt may backfire if the other one simply becomes triumphant and takes on no blame whatsoever. This may lead
the one who took the blame to regret having done so, and the quarrel
may flare up again. Even if the quarrel is not reopened, a repeated
pattern of one person taking the blame may lead to a gradual deterio-
ration of the relationship, depending on the reality of the accusations.
If both participants, and others, agree that one of the participants *is*
habitually to blame (never keeping his or her promises, always being
unfaithful, or drinking too much), the burden of guilt is accumulating
toward some peak. If the guilt really is seen as shared, the one who is
admitting guilt may teach the other one to follow the same strategy. In
this case quarreling may gradually diminish.

5. A compromise strategy is to suggest that the blame must be shared,
or alternatively that there is no one to blame, or that someone else is
to blame. Common to these strategies is the establishment of *equality*
between the two participants. They are easy to initiate, but may not
work, because the other one may be unwilling to accept any blame at
all, or may be unwilling to free the opponent of any guilt.

6. A primitive, but not unknown, strategy is to use brute force either
physically through hurting and even killing the adversary, or through
threatening to do so, or to take other destructive action. This strategy
may be used to silence the adversary, but is itself an instance of unre-
spectable behavior, leading to additional feelings of guilt. It also leads
to irreparable damage of the relationship, leaving fear, anger, and loa-
thing in its wake. The number of possible moves in quarrels is very
limited, and the analysis presented here pretty much exhausts them.
Given information about the participants and the situation, predictability may be quite good.

Case 7.3.3 ***P* wants to give *Q* a gift in order to make *Q* happy.** In principle, the
presentation of a gift always has a double goal. It is intended to com-
municate the care of a person for another and it is intended to make
the receiver happy, also through the specific properties of the gift.
These two goals are to some extent interdependent because, if care is
not communicated, this may detract from the happiness of the receiver and if the qualities of the gift in itself create no happiness, this may
lower the likelihood that the gift was given out of care, as seen from
the perspective of the receiver. A limited number of factors are involved. First, there is the *occasion* for the gift. If the occasion is such
that the giver *ought to* give a gift, the motivation, as seen by the receiver becomes ambiguous. It is unclear to what extent the gift was given
because *P cares* for *Q* and, hence, wanted to make *Q* happy, or because *P had to* give the gift because of the occasion. Since *Q* wants to

believe what is the case (Axiom 2.4.2), *Q* will be motivated to ascertain what motivated the gift. On the other hand, *Q* may have reasons for **not** wanting to know this, notably because *Q* is afraid that the reason for the gift may have been purely conventional, and *Q* wants to avoid knowing this for certain. The strength of a feeling is equal to the product of the strength of the want and the strength of the belief involved (Definition 3.3.1), and, hence, certain knowledge of something painful is more painful than a mere suspicion. (If the likelihood is already very high, and the pain expected is very strong, the certainty of something painful may come as a relief. The explanation of this is that the want to know is satisfied, and that the exertion involved in alternating between hope and despair is eliminated.) Another source of ambiguity for the receiver is the case where it appears that the donor may have some *other* motive than care, even though the occasion does not call for a gift. Obviously, a suspicion that the gift is intended to bribe or soften the receiver may detract from the resulting happiness.

The preceding means that, whereas the receiver has the cognitive task of ascertaining exactly *why* the gift was given, the donor has the task of presenting the gift in such a way that the *intended message,* whatever it is, is received. A typical task for a donor is to convey some degree of care, even though the situation is a conventional one, and/or there may be possible ulterior motives. Obviously, the situation is more simple if the occasion is *not* a conventional one and if there are *no* easily conceivable ulterior motives. In these cases, the receiver almost *has* to interpret the gift as being given out of care. The main options for the donor lie (a) in the choice of gift; and (b) in the way it is presented. Since the gift is intended to convey care, it should make *Q* happy.

Several considerations are pertinent in this connection. First, the very presentation of a gift on an occasion when a gift shall be presented means that *respect* is conveyed, and this, in itself, should make the receiver somewhat happy, since persons want to be respected (Theorem 5.2.3). A second consideration has to do with *what* makes *Q* happy. If *P* knows what makes *Q* happy, this may be an indication for *Q* that *P* cares, because if *P* cares for *Q,* then *P* will be interested in finding out what makes *Q* happy (Corollary 5.3.1). However, the way *P* comes to know about what makes *Q* happy is quite important here. If *P* asks *Q* or friends of *Q,* this is somewhat ambiguous, because although it may indicate genuine caring it is also an easy way to simulate caring. If, on the other hand, *P* finds a gift that makes *Q* very happy indeed, and *P* could only have found it through a very keen understanding of *Q* and/or through an extraordinary expenditure of time and effort, this will serve as a pretty convincing evidence of *P*'s care for *Q.* If the gift does not make *Q* happy, yet obviously is the outcome of extraordinary efforts, it may still convey the message of care, which, again, may outweigh the disappointment with respect to the specific properties of the presented gift. A gift which, in itself, may not make *Q* particularly happy, may still be taken to indicate care, notably in a context where there are many other indications of this. *P* may have traveled far and at inconvenient times to present the gift, or the relationship between *P* and *Q* is such that *Q* already believes that *P* cares. In this case, the gift is interpreted as indicating care, even though neither the circumstances nor the gift in itself contribute to this.

The choice of gift is always a delicate one. If it is very expensive, and if *P* believes that *Q* believes that *P* has modest economic means, it may serve the purpose of showing that *P* is willing to suffer some hardship in order to make *Q* happy. On the other hand, an expensive gift may serve to emphasize a possible difference between *P* and *Q* in economic means which is unfortunate since it forces *Q* to reciprocate in style at a later occasion. This is the case when *P* is very wealthy and *Q* is very poor. If, under these circumstances, *P* chooses to give *Q* a very expensive gift, the outcome depends on the way this is understood by *Q*. If *Q* believes that *P* has done this knowingly and does not expect any expensive gift in return, this may be OK. If *Q* believes that *P* has not thought about the difference in economic means or that *P* believes that *Q* is wealthy, the situation becomes very difficult. If it is not suitable to talk about economic means, *Q* may be forced to find a gift that is not too different in value from the one received from *P*. On the other hand, if *P* gives *Q* a gift which is too cheap, this may convey precisely the impression that this is an unimportant matter and that *P* has not been willing to use money for this purpose. Obviously, the message depends on how *Q* sees *P*'s economy. If the gift reveals a glaring lack of knowledge of *Q*'s existing possessions or of *Q*'s artistic/esthetic views, this reinforces the impression that the gift is only motivated by convention. This is so because if *P* really cared for *Q* it would be expected that *P* had acquired some knowledge about *Q* and *Q*'s lot (Corollary 5.3.1). Again, the presentation (and exchange) of gifts involves a limited number of variables, and, given knowledge about the donor and the recipient, as well as of their situations, the possibility of predicting outcomes is relatively good.

Case 7.3.4 **Hiding a secret. *P* wants to hide *X* from *Q*.** Two concrete examples may be thought of as illustrating the general principles. (a) *X* is a drug habit that the youth *P* has, and *Q* is a parent; (b) *X* is an ongoing affair that *P* has, and *P* and *Q* are a married couple. In both cases, *P* wants *Q* to take for granted that *not-X* is the case. The optimal strategy for *P* is to try to prevent any event that is likely to make *Q* cease taking *not-X* for granted. In other words, *P* tries to prevent *Q* from becoming *suspicious* (Definition 3.5.31). If *P* becomes suspicious that something is not what it seems to be, it follows from this and from Axiom 2.4.2 ("*P* wants to believe what is the case"), that *Q* will want to know what is going on. The task of hiding something from a suspicious person is much more difficult than hiding it from an unsuspicious person because the former will actively try to find out. If *Q* has become suspicious, the goal for *P* cannot merely be to continue to hide *X*, because this would only prolong a difficult and unstable situation (*Q* being continuously suspicious). The goal must be to allay the suspicions, which is generally very difficult. The reason for this difficulty is that, whereas the unsuspicious person needs no proof or evidence whatsoever, the suspicious person needs completely convincing evidence in order to come to believe that his or her fears were entirely unfounded.

In the first example, concerning the drug habit, repeatedly negative blood tests, coupled with practically complete knowledge of what the youth is doing around the clock, combined with strong evidence for other interests and a completely negative attitude toward drugs might allay the fears of the parent. Similarly, in the second case (the illicit affair), knowledge that the suspected lover had in fact been in South America during the entire relevant period, coupled with other consistent evidence, could lead *P* to give up the suspicions. However, in real life, the available evidence very frequently retains at least some ambiguity, and, therefore, suspicions, once awakened, often tend to linger on, at least in the form of a somewhat heightened selective awareness of relevant events.

Persons who have experienced early and massive betrayal in some form may retain a generalized tendency to be suspicious and a very high readiness to develop specific suspicions. This is sometimes called "paranoia" or being „paranoid." Encountering such persons involves a problem that is the inverse of the one of hiding something from someone who is suspicious. This is the problem of convincing someone that the suspicions are in fact unfounded. The correct and natural strategy of meeting a suspicious person, when you are innocent, is to be very open and honest and provide the person with as much evidence as possible. This may work on one occasion, but, if repeated, it may become a strenuous burden on the other person who will become occupied with continuously providing what he or she thinks is superfluous evidence of innocence. Also the very activity of attempting to prove innocence may itself be interpreted as an indication of guilt.

In order to hide *X* effectively from *Q* (or in order to make sure that *Q* does not develop any unfounded suspicions), *P* must be very much aware of *Q*'s wants, beliefs, dispositions, and routines. In particular, *P* must be highly sensitive to whether or not, and in what way, *Q* is suspicious at any given time. As long as *Q* is not suspicious, it is enough to make sure that no events likely to evoke suspicion occur. If, on the other hand, suspicion has arisen, a state of emergency exists, and *P* must be extremely careful in dealing with *Q*. *P* must behave in every way as an innocent person, while *Q* is extremely sensitive to any deviation from a natural pattern. For instance, overplaying and overemphasizing will be immediately detected. ("The lady doth protest too much".) Conversely, having become suspicious, the best strategy for *Q* is to *hide* this from *P* because, if *P* senses the suspicion, he or she will become alert and redouble the efforts to hide *X* and allay all suspicions. If *Q* is really suspicious, but appears to be totally unsuspecting, *P* will relax and be more likely to make a slip. In general, then, secrets tend to remain hidden if the bearer succeeds in not awakening the slightest suspicion in the other person. This can, typically, only be achieved if the person who harbors a secret is very sensitive to what goes on in the other person. It is self-evident that ongoing, habitual patterns of events are most difficult to hide since they have so many implications and consequences in everyday life. Relatively brief and past events (such as a brief period of drug abuse or a brief affair) may be relatively safely stored, and the need to guard them becomes smaller as time passes and the number of occasions related to them diminishes. The theme of trust vs. suspicion is a central one in human life, and, as in the preceding examples, there are only a limited number of types of options and moves available to the participants.

Case 7.3.5 Conversation. *P* and *Q* are having lunch together. They know each other quite well. They happen to sit together and there is no preagreed agendum. Both consider briefly and probably mostly unreflectively what to talk about. In the given type of situation one is *supposed to* talk, and this norm is always adhered to. *P*'s decision about topic *must* be a function of the following four variables: (a) what interests and is salient for *P*; (b) what *P* believes may interest *Q*; (c) what *P* wants to and is willing to talk about with *Q*; (d) what *P* believes *Q* wants and is willing to talk about with *P*. Implicit in the formulations "interests" and "wants to" is that *P* and *Q* *know* something about the themes. One cannot want to talk about something one cannot talk about because none of the participants knows anything about it. *P* or *Q* may want to talk about a topic he or she does not know anything about, *if* he or she believes that the other is knowledgeable in this field or *if* he or she believes that something valuable may nevertheless ensue from the conversation. There are also many topics about which *P* does not want to talk with *Q* because they are seen as too "private," or because *P* does not trust *Q* in these matters, or because *P* does not think that anything interesting will ensue from the conversation. Similarly there are topics about which *P* believes that *Q* may not be willing to talk for similar kinds of reasons. The better *P* and *Q* know each other, the better they are able to judge what themes are appropriate to talk about.

97

This also means that when *P* and *Q* are approximate strangers, there is a clear tendency to select relatively innoccuous themes and to treat them very tentatively until signals are forthcoming about their appropriateness. *P* starts talking about theme *X* before *Q* has had time to introduce theme *Y.* If *Q* is sufficiently interested in bringing up *Y,* he or she may shelve it on "immediate access," that is, wait for an opportunity to bring it up. When *P* has introduced *X, Q* is *obligated* to answer or comment on that theme. *Q*'s contribution must be classifiable as a response to *P*'s introduction and cannot be unrelated to it. If the response appears to be unrelated, it must be interpreted by *P* in one of four ways: (a) *Q* cannot have heard correctly what *P* said; (b) *Q* must have misunderstood what *P* said; (c) *P* cannot have heard correctly what *Q* answered; or (d) *P* must have misunderstood *Q*'s answer. As a last resort and under very special conditions, it may also be possible that *Q* has deliberately misheard or ignored what *P* said. This final possibility means that *Q* does not show respect for *P* and, hence, may make *P* angry, cf. the conditions of anger (Definition 3.5.5). If *P* believes that *Q* must have heard correctly what was said and that *Q* could not possibly have misinterpreted it, *P* has a reason to believe that *Q* deliberately misheard and ignored what was said.

However, normally, disrespectful behavior is not displayed. Hence, there is a choice between believing that something was not heard correctly and that it was misunderstood. The differential diagnosis is usually easy. *P* may repeat what was said in such a way that *Q* ought to hear it (stronger voice, clearer pronunciation, moving closer). If *Q* can now repeat what was said or responds adequately, it becomes reasonable to assume that the problem lies in faulty hearing. If *Q* still gives evidence of not hearing, under conditions that in the view of *P* are perfectly normal, *P* may come to entertain the hypothesis that *Q* is indeed hard of hearing, and may start to adjust his or her voice to this. If *Q* repeats what *P* said correctly and still responds in an apparently irrelevant manner, *P*'s remaining hypothesis is that there is some misunderstanding. *P* will then proceed to check this through elaborating some of the equivalences, implications, negations, and irrelevancies of the statement, see the definition of understanding of what is said or done (5.4.0). *P* will say, "what I meant was ..." (equivalent formulation), or "It follows from what I said that ..." (implication), or "I am denying that ..." (negation), or "What I said has nothing whatsoever to do with ..." (irrelevance). This gives *Q* an opportunity to compare the statements with those that follow from his or her interpretation of what *P* said. The process may go on for a briefer or longer period of time, and *Q* may reciprocate by saying, "As I understood you, you were saying that ..." (equivalence), "It follows from what you said ..." (implication), "You denied that ..." (negation), or "What you said had nothing to do with ..." (irrelevance).

The proportion of a conversation taken up with attempts to clarify apparent misunderstandings varies tremendously. In teenagers, and adults too, there sometimes occurs an intentional sabotage of communication. In order not to be persuaded from a position experienced as weak, one may choose to interpret the other person's statements in ways suitable for one's own purpose and with complete disregard for what may have been intended. By means of this strategy one avoids being drawn into a real exchange and, thereby, being influenced by the other one. One also achieves a conversation which is almost completely taken up with futile attempts to clarify a web of misunderstandings and which frequently results in the other person giving up. "It is hopeless to talk with you," "You do not listen to me," "You keep on misrepresenting what I say," and so on. The absence of an intention to understand is a certain sign that one has reached a rigid barrier that cannot, for the time being, be traversed.

After a while, conversing about topic X, Q may want to switch to topic Y. This is permissible only under certain conditions which are quite definite, but hard to formulate explicitly. One obvious condition is the one where topic X appears to be exhausted, and there is a relatively clear pause. Another is when P's interest in X does not appear to Q to be very strong. Q may also explicitly state that he or she would very much like to talk a little about Y, if X is temporarily exhausted or if it is OK for P, etc. Another, very frequent way is to change the topic surreptitiously, at a point when what is said can be interpreted as belonging to both topic X and topic Y. This interpretation can be allowed to be rather far-fetched, especially if Q does not think that topic X is very important to P. If it is, and Q attempts to change the topic, this may be taken as disrespect (and sometimes lack of care) on the part of Q. A frequent maneuver is to say, "That reminds me of . . .," where what it reminds of is something within topic Y. If P follows this (does not resist, for example by saying, "Let me return to what we were talking about a little while ago"), the topic has now changed to Y. Conversations vary tremendously in the rigidity with which themes are maintained, the important variables being the external frame of reference of the conversation and the interest of the themes to the participants.

Case 7.3.6 **Persuasion. P wants to persuade Q to change her/his mind about X.** There are two different basic tasks involved in persuasion corresponding to the two basic categories of wants and beliefs. P may want to change Q from (a) wanting X to not wanting X; or from (b) not wanting X to wanting X; similarly, P may want to persuade Q (c) to believe in X; or (d) to not believe in X. All four tasks involve a limited set of clear alternatives. In order to get Q to stop wanting X, P must get Q to believe that relatively less pleasure or more pain will ensue from getting X than Q had believed before. This may refer specifically to the achievement of X or to concomitant or subsequent consequences of achieving X compared to alternative goals. The task may be achieved either through verbal communication, oral or written, where it is important that the sources of the communication are believed by Q to be *credible*, or through arranging experiences of achieving X, where the actual pleasure is lowered or the pain is heightened compared to what was expected by Q. In the latter case, it is important to have Q believe that the experience has been representative (typical) of what may be expected in the future. If Q has wanted to visit a particular scenic point and it is foggy, the want to repeat the visit will depend on what credible information is given about the likelihood of fog at that spot. If Q is told by an expert that the place is foggy 99% of the year, the want to repeat the attempt will be lower than if Q is told by the expert that he or she has been unlucky as the spot is foggy only about 1% of the year. Obviously, the preceding is also valid when Q does not actually visit the place, but is only informed about it by the expert.

The credibility of an informant is similarly dependent either on indirect evidence about that credibility or on direct experiences where the informant's statements turned out to be correct. If a person whom Q regards as highly credible vouches for the expert's credibility this may have a strong effect. Conversely, if a highly credible person expresses doubts about an informant's credibility, this will be correspondingly weakened. The example of the scenic spot may obviously be reversed. If the person visits the spot on a sunny day with a lovely view, the want to repeat the visit will be strengthened if a credible informant says that 99 days out of 100 are sunny than if the informant states that Q has been very lucky because only one day out of 100 is sunny.

In general, both wants and beliefs are changed through manipulations on beliefs. These may, however, involve two kinds of changes, namely of likelihoods and of amounts of pleasure/pain. The manipulations on likelihood involve higher degrees of likelihood, such as credibility, which is a second-order likelihood that a first-order likelihood is what it seems to be. In evaluating a complicated context, Q may evaluate the mutual interplay of many cues or indicators of likelihood. In order for P to persuade Q about something, it is necessary for P to have an adequate degree of *understanding* of Q's wants and beliefs in the relevant area, including the likely effect of various kinds of information and direct experience. It may be said that if P understands Q perfectly and if P has control over the various possibilities of influencing Q, then there is a maximum likelihood that P will succeed in persuading Q. However, it should be added that P's understanding of Q must include an understanding of Q's possible want *not* to be persuaded. If there, for Q, is pain in being persuaded, the task is even more difficult. If the pain has to do with the fact that Q must give up a position defended against P, P may circumvent this through making it appear that *P* has nothing to do with the change and/or that *P* is actually against the change. In every case of persuasion or teaching, the practician must take into account the following general principle:

Axiom 7.3.7 **A person's belief system will change in the least extensive way possible, which is taken by that person to be compatible with a perceived inconsistency.**

Note 7.3.8 Example: *P* is convinced that there are no unicorns. *P* then sees a unicorn in the garden. The least extensive interpretation of this is that this is a simple misperception due to the unfavorable perceptual conditions involved. If the unicorn still appears to be there, with the garden lights on, the next hypothesis may be that someone has somehow designed a fake unicorn as a practical joke. It is simply a statue of a unicorn. However, if the creature moves about, this does not work, and the next interpretation is that someone has disguised some other animal as a unicorn. If a closer inspection fails to substantiate this, *P* may resort to the assumption that this is a mutation of some other species, such as an antelope or goat of some kind. This interpretation still safeguards *P*'s general views of the natural order of organisms. If a closer examination indicates that this creature does not belong to any known species, it may still be seen as some kind of weird mutation. However, *P* may also start to wonder about her or his own state of mind. "Am I dreaming, is this an hallucination?" If, finally, the creature starts to speak and to dance in the air, the interpretation may force itself upon *P,* who will by then have become pretty upset, that this may be a genuine unicorn. However, this entails a complete breakdown of *P*'s system of beliefs about the world and will not come about easily. At some early stage in the preceding sequence, *P* is certain to have appealed to *others*. If these fail to corroborate *P*'s impression of seeing the unicorn, it is categorized as an hallucination of some kind. On the other hand, if others corroborate *P*'s experiences, this makes them much more real and less frightening. For a lone person to experience an apparently genuine unicorn would be extremely frightening, but if many persons share this experience completely, it would simply mean a dramatic change and a threat to earlier views, but not nearly as frightening. Commonality is the most important building block of reality, especially if there has been no mutual influence. Scientific psychologists, too, rely heavily on intercorrelations of judgments of *independent* observers.

Note 7.3.9 Given the preceding, the task of persuasion becomes very difficult. The person to be persuaded will interpret all contrary evidence in ways which change her or his belief system as little as possible. Often, the belief system will be such that all evidence may be incorporated, and no contrary data have any impact. In that case, the summoning of support may be the best way. If credible others accept the contrary evidence, the person will have problems in resisting and will have to find plausible explanations for why other, normally credible, persons are fooled. Typically, the person threatened by heavy persuasion will also look for supporters. In typical cases, persuasion efforts of a brief dramatic kind are doomed. Discussions and disputations normally end with a draw, particularly when the very act of letting oneself be persuaded is taken to have a negative value. On the other hand, there may be a slow erosion of defenses if the balance of the arguments and observations favor an alternative view and if one can defect with one's "face" preserved.

Note 7.3.10   The task of the skilled persuader is hard. In order to have any hope at all, one must, normally, understand very well the beliefs and wants of the person involved as well as the relevant context and surrounding persons. Given this the possibilities and impossibilities of the task should become clear. There is a parallel here to the case of suspiciousness. As long as the persuader does not make the victim aware of the issue, the task is much easier. Evidence may be presented in seemingly unintended ways, perhaps unrelated to the persuader. Contrary evidence may be similarly discredited. Ethical issues are also relevant here, such as was the case with the subliminal pictures flashed in connection with advertisements.

Note 7.3.11   The series of cases ends arbitrarily at this point. A main reason for this is that there is a factor of diminishing return as the system is repeatedly and more or less explicitly applied to new contents. As these analyses are repeated, the way they are conducted should become clearer, and a reader should become able to continue on his or her own.

Summary

While a full expansion of the system permits analyses of the interaction of three or more persons, only two-person interactions are treated in this chapter. "Interaction between two persons" is defined as the mutual taking into account of the other one's acts in one's own acting. Three main types of interaction are introduced, namely *cooperation, consultation,* and *coercion.* In cooperation both participants have low own-control and high other-control, in consultation both have high own-control and low other-control, and in coercion one participant has high own-control and high other-control whereas the other has low own-control and low other-control. The following cases of interaction are analyzed in some detail: *P* is happy and *Q* is bored, *P* and *Q* are angry at each other, *P* wants to give *Q* a gift, *P* wants to hide a secret from *Q*, *P* and *Q* converse with no preagreed agendum, *P* wants to persuade *Q* about something.

8 Epilogue

The system presented here raises at least three fundamental questions, namely whether it is transcultural, whether it is stable, and how it connects with the empirical tradition in psychology. I will try to offer some tentative answers to each one of them.

8.1 Is the System Transcultural?

In order to answer this question, an explicit and precise definition of "transcultural" is needed. One plausible formulation is that a system is transcultural to the extent that it can be applied to and is valid in other cultures with other languages. In this connection, the question of translatability becomes central. An exact translation of the system means that the relations between its propositions remain unchanged both with respect to formal logic and with respect to consensus among informants. Suppose that E_1 and E_2 are propositions belonging to the present English version, that T_1 and T_2 are the corresponding propositions in another language, and that E_1RE_2 (E_1 and E_2 have the relation R) is valid in the English version. The validity means that informants agree that E_1RE_2 is the case, and this can also be proved through formal logic, given definitions acceptable to all informants. Given the above, there is exact translatability in this respect if T_1RT_2 is valid, that is if all informants agree that T_1RT_2 is the case, and this can be proved through formal logic, given definitions acceptable to all informants.

It follows from the above that the question of translatability is an open one and can only be answered concretely for each pair of propositions in each pair of languages. In view of the relatively high approximate translatability among most human languages, it may perhaps be surmised that the present system is at least approximately transcultural. Obviously, it may be that it will be more or less elegant and appealing in different languages. In general, exact answers will only be forthcoming when translations are actually attempted.

One interesting subquestion concerns the notion of time. This notion is certainly differently structured in societies where watches and clocks are common and in those without any chronological instrumentation. The present system should have no difficulty in this respect since it presupposes no measurement of time, beyond the fixation of an instant or period (now), and the relations of earlier (past), and later (future), in other words, *simultaneity* and *succession*.

8.2 Is the System Stable?

It is well known that cultures and their languages change over time. It should also be clear that the problem of translatability is the same between two contemporary cultures as it is between the same culture at an earlier and at a later time. Concretely, this is manifested, for example, in problems of communication between two generations when change has been particularly rapid. There are two reasons for believing that the present system must be relatively stable. The first is that societal changes must always involve considerable translatability in order to preserve the conditions for orderly interaction and communication. The second is that the concepts described in the present system appear to be of such a fundamental nature that it is hard to see how they could change very much. However, the conclusion must be the same as in the question of cross-culturality, namely that stability must be investigated in actual cases.

8.3 How Does the System Relate to the Empirical Tradition in Psychology?

The answer to this question, as I see it, is that the present system relates to psychological realities in the same way as geometry relates to physical realities, that is, geography. The location and form of an object is characterized by its geometrically expressed relations to other objects and to a coordinate system. But the actual discovery of the object was an empirical geographical one. Similarly, the activity of a person is characterized through the present system of psycho-logic in relation to contexts (including other persons) as well as in relation to the normative system of the surrounding culture, and so on. However, the mapping of the actual activity of this person is an empirical psychological one.

The formal analogy between geometry and psycho-logic holds up in every respect. Each new geographical location is mapped geometrically, and each new person is described in terms of psycho-logic. Geometry and psycho-logic are conceptual systems in terms of which we *must* describe, respectively, the spatial and the psychological world. The systems themselves are relatively removed from empirical testing, but, because of the built-in constraints, they generate many predictions. If the predictions fail, this is invariably attributed to insufficient or faulty information rather than to the formal propositions involved.

The metatheoretical problems debated in the case of geometry no doubt also exist in psycho-logic. However, whatever the outcome of these debates will be, it will not lead to the abandonment of either geometry or psycho-logic. As far as the latter is concerned, one cannot describe a human being who is not a person, one cannot describe a person who does not have wants and beliefs, one cannot describe a want without a goal, a belief without a content, and so on. Scientific psychology must capitalize on these constraints. How to proceed from then on is another and open question.

Appendix 1 Definitions of the System

1 Being Aware and Active

being aware of 1.1.0
being conscious 1.1.5
acting 1.2.0
acting overtly 1.2.4
acting covertly 1.2.5
relevance 1.2.9
taking into account 1.2.13
being reflectively aware of 1.3.0
being unreflectively aware of 1.3.1
acting reflectively 1.3.10
acting unreflectively 1.3.13
person 1.4.0
human psychology 1.4.6
context 1.5.5
remembering reflectively 1.6.1
remembering unreflectively 1.6.4
forgetting at reflective level 1.6.6
forgetting at unreflective level 1.6.9
perceiving reflectively 1.6.12
perceiving unreflectively 1.6.15
expecting reflectively 1.6.18
expecting unreflectively 1.6.21

2 Wanting and Believing

want 2.1.0
being reflectively aware of want 2.1.3
being unreflectively aware of want 2.1.7
strength of want 2.1.14
conflict of wants 2.1.16
compatibility of wants 2.1.25

pleasure 2.2.0
pain 2.2.2
fulfillment of want 2.2.23
frustration of want 2.2.24
belief 2.3.0
reality 2.3.2
believing reflectively 2.3.6
believing unreflectively 2.3.11
strength of belief 2.3.17
conflict of beliefs 2.3.18

3 Feeling

feeling 3.1.1
reflective feeling 3.2.2
unreflective feeling 3.2.3
partly reflective feeling 3.2.13
strength of feeling 3.3.1
relative strength of feeling 3.3.7
conflict of feelings 3.3.8
happiness 3.4.2
degree of happiness 3.4.3
boredom 3.5.2
anger 3.5.5
fear 3.5.12
shame 3.5.16
guilt 3.5.19
sadness 3.5.23
depression 3.5.26
envy 3.5.29
suspicion 3.5.31
disgust 3.5.34

4 Acting

relative ability 4.2.2
relative difficulty 4.2.4
highest expected utility 4.3.2

5 Characteristics of Persons

respect 5.2.0
care 5.3.0
understanding what 5.4.0 and 7.1.5
understanding why 5.4.2 and 7.1.6
control 5.5.0
own-control 5.5.6
other-control 5.5.8
self-control 5.5.10
psychological proposition 5.7.1
valid psychological proposition 5.7.3

6 Personal Change

first-order change 6.1.0
second-order change 6.1.2
mental problem 6.2.10

7 Interacting

interaction 7.1.0
understanding what 7.1.5
understanding why 7.1.6
conversation 7.1.11
talking to 7.1.12
listening to 7.1.13
cooperation 7.2.1
consultation 7.2.4
coercion 7.2.6
conflict 7.2.9

Appendix 2 Axioms of the System

1.2.7 A conscious person is continuously acting.

1.3.4 A person can describe that of which he or she is reflectively aware and only that.

1.3.21 Reflective awareness defines an object of awareness.

1.5.0 A person's awareness and acting tend to be completely integrated (unitary).

2.2.17 The strength of a person's want of X is directly proportional to the amount of increment in pleasure or decrement in pain that the person believes will occur when X is attained.

2.2.26 If two pleasures/pains, P_1 and P_2, occur at the same time, they combine in such a way that $P_1 \& P_2 > P_1$, and $P_1 \& P_2 > P_2$.

2.3.20 The strength of a person's belief that X is the case is directly proportional to that person's estimate of the likelihood that X is the case.

2.4.2 A person wants to believe what is the case.

2.5.1 A person is held responsible and accountable for his or her acts by everyone involved.

2.5.5 A person wants to do what he or she believes is morally right and wants not to do what he or she believes is morally wrong.

2.5.7 A person wants everyone to accept what he or she believes is morally right and to reject what he or she believes is morally wrong.

3.1.5 The sum of the strengths of a person's feelings at a given moment has an upper limit equal to the maximum possible strength of any single feeling at that moment.

4.1.0 A person P does A in the context C at time t if, and only if, P can do A in C at t and P tries to do A in C at t.

4.2.0 A person P can do A in the context C at time t if, and only if, P's ability to do A in C at t exceeds the difficulty of doing A in C at t.

4.2.7 **The degree of exertion of a person P in performing A in the context C at time t is inversely proportional to the size of the positive difference between the ability of P to perform A in C at t and the difficulty for P of A in C at t.**

4.3.1 **A person P tries to do A in a context C at time t if, and only if, A is the act which, for P in C at t, has the highest expected utility.**

4.3.5 **A person wants to minimize exertion.**

5.3.7 **Every person wants to be cared for by someone and wants to care for someone.**

5.6.1 **Every person reflectively believes that he or she exists.**

5.6.5 **Every person wants to continue to exist.**

5.7.6 **For every valid psychological proposition X, there exists a valid psychological proposition Y, where $Y=$ "Every person takes it for granted that X is valid for every person."**

5.7.8 **For every valid psychological proposition X, there exists a valid psychological proposition Z, where $Z=$ "Every person takes it for granted that every person takes it for granted that X is valid for every person."**

5.7.10 **For every valid psychological proposition X, there exists a valid psychological proposition V, where $V=$ "Every person takes it for granted that every person takes it for granted that every other person also takes it for granted that the proposition X applies to every person."**

6.1.5 **Discrimination and differentiation are irreversible.**

6.1.7 **A person's awareness of the future consists of extrapolations from that person's awareness of trends in the past.**

7.3.7 **A person's belief system will change in the least extensive way possible, which is taken by that person to be compatible with a perceived inconsistency.**

Appendix 3 Some Earlier Presentations, Critiques, and Replies Concerning the Present Type of Approach

Bandura, A. (1978) On distinguishing between logical and empirical verification. A comment on Smedslund. *Scandinavian Journal of Psychology, 19,* 97-99.

Jones A. J. I. (1980) Psychology and "ordinary language" – a critique of Smedslund. *Scandinavian Journal of Psychology, 21,* 225-229.

Lock, A. (1981) Indigenous psychology and human nature: A psychological perspective. In P. Heelas & A. Lock (Eds.) *Indigenous psychologies: The anthropology of the self.* London: Academic.

Shotter, J. & Burton, M. (1983) Common sense accounts of human action: The descriptive formulations of Heider, Smedslund, and Ossorio. In L. Wheeler (Ed.) *Review of Personality and Social Psychology,* Vol. 4. Beverly Hills, CA: Sage

Sjoberg, L. (1982) Logical versus psychological necessity: A discussion of the role of common sense in psychological theory. *Scandinavian Journal of Psychology, 23,* 65-78.

Smedslund, J. (1970) Circular relation between understanding and logic. *Scandinavian Journal of Psychology, 11,* 217-219.

Smedslund, J. (1978) Bandura's theory of self-efficacy: A set of common sense theorems. *Scandinavian Journal of Psychology, 19,* 1-14.

Smedslund, J. (1978) Some psychological theories are not empirical: Reply to Bandura. *Scandinavian Journal of Psychology, 19,* 101-102.

Smedslund, J. (1979) Between the analytic and the arbitrary: A case study of psychological research. *Scandinavian Journal of Psychology, 20,* 1-12.

Smedslund, J. (1980) Analyzing the primary code: From empiricism to apriorism. In D. R. Olson (Ed.) *The social foundations of language and thought: Essays in honor of Jerome S. Bruner* (pp. 47-73). New York: Norton.

Smedslund, J. (1981) From ordinary to scientific language: Reply to Jones. *Scandinavian Journal of Psychology, 21,* 231-233.

Smedslund, J. (1981) The logic of psychological treatment. *Scandinavian Journal of Psychology, 22,* 65-77.

Smedslund, J. (1982) Common sense as psychosocial reality: A reply to Sjoberg. *Scandinavian Journal of Psychology, 23,* 79-82.

Smedslund, J. (1982) Seven common sense rules of psychological treatment. *Journal of the Norwegian Psychological Association, 19,* 441-449.

Smedslund, J. (1982) Revising explications of common sense through dialogue: Thirtysix psychological theorems. *Scandinavian Journal of Psychology, 23,* 299-305.

Smedslund, J. (1984) The invisible obvious: Culture in psychology. In K. M. J. Lagerspetz & P. Niemi (Eds.) *Psychology in the 1990's.* (pp. 443-452) Amsterdam: Elsevier

Smedslund, J. (1984) What is necessarily true in psychology? In J. R. Royce & L. P. Mos (Eds.) *Annals of Theoretical Psychology. 2,* 241-272.

Smedslund, J. (1984) Psychology cannot take leave of common sense: Reply to Tennesen, Vollmer, and Wilkes. In J. R. Royce & L. P. Mos (Eds.) *Annals of Theoretical Psychology, 2,* 295-302.

Smedslund, J. (1985). Necessarily true cultural psychologies. In K. J. Gergen & K. E. Davis (Eds.) *The social construction of the person* (pp. 73-87). Berlin, Heidelberg, New York: Springer.

Smedslund, J. (1986). The explication of psychological common sense: Implications for the science of psychology. In R. Barcan Marcus et al. (Eds.) *Logic, methodology and philosophy of science VII* (pp. 481-494). Amsterdam: Elsevier

Smedslund, J. (1986). How stable is common sense psychology and can it be transcended? Reply to Valsiner. *Scandinavian Journal of Psychology, 27,* 91–94.

Smedslund, J. (1987a). Das Beschreiben von Beschreibungen., Erklären von Erklärungen und Vorhersagen von Vorhersagen: Paradigmatische Fälle für die Psychologie. In J. Brandtstädter (Ed.) *Struktur und Erfahrung in der psychologischen Forschung,* Berlin: Gruyter, 159–168.

Smedslund, J. (1987b). The epistemic status of interitem correlations in Eysenck's Personality Questionnaire: The a priori versus the empirical in psychological data. *Scandinavian Journal of Psychology, 28,* 42–55.

Smedslund, J. (1987c). Ebbinghaus the illusionist: How psychology came to look like an experimental science. In *Passauer Schriften zur Psychologiegeschichte, 5,* Ebbinghaus-Studien *2,* 225–239.

Tennesen, H. (1984). What is remarkable in psychology? In J. R. Royce & L. P. Mos (Eds.) *Annals of Theoretical Psychology, 2,* 273–278.

Valsiner, J. (1985). Common sense and psychological theories: The historical nature of logical necessity. *Scandinavian Journal of Psychology, 26,* 97–109.

Vollmer, F. (1984). On the limitations of commonsense psychology. In J. R. Royce & L. P. Mos (Eds.) *Annals of Theoretical Psychology, 2,* 279–286.

Wilkes, K. V. (1984). It ain't necessarily so. In J. R. Royce & L. P. Mos (Eds.) *Annals of Theoretical Psychology, 2,* 287–294.